ty

Born illegitimate in 1928, **Sheila Stewart** counted herself lucky to have been brought up by the Waifs and Strays Society. After a career in teaching she published her autobiography *A Home From Home* in 1968. Several short stories and radio plays followed. A radio script based on her book *Country Kate* won the Writers' Guild of Great Britain Award for 1974. After nursing her elderly mother-in-law for several years she began writing again with *Lifting the Latch* (Oxford University Press, 1987). For five years until 1992, she researched and wrote *Ramlin Rose,* which looks at the life of a working narrow boat woman and her family. The manuscript of this book, *Toby of the White City,* also based on a working boat family, followed a few years later, but it was never published during the author's lifetime. The family released this book in 2023 for publication.

Sheila Stewart, who died in 2014, was married to Eric, and had three children; she lived latterly in a village in Warwickshire.

Toby of the White City

The Boat Dog's Story

CANALBOOKSHOP

Toby of the White City

The Boat Dog's Story

SHEILA STEWART

Illustrated by David 'Dusty' Miller

CanalBookShop

First published 2024 by
CanalBookShop
www.canalbookshop.co.uk

Printed in the UK

ISBN 978-1-7399896-4-4

Alfred Hone's horse-drawn boat Rose and Betty *at Banbury, 1946 photographed by Angela Rolt. © Tim Rolt*

CONTENTS

Drawing of Toby on White City
by Denys Watkins-Pitchford - 'BB'
(Part of a larger image published in
LTC Rolt's 'Narrow Boat' of 1944)

The Midlands Canal System Circa 1900
Liverpool
Man Ship C
Manchester
Bridgewater Canal
Chester
Northwich
Sheffield
Macclesfield Canal
Shropshire Union Canal
Stoke-on-Trent
River Trent
Trent & Mersey Canal
Derby
Nottingham
Wolverhampton
B'ham
Canal
Nav
Coventry Canal
Ashby Canal
Leicester Navigation
Birmingham
Warwick & B'ham
Stourport
Worcs & B'ham Canal
Coventry
Grand Junc Canal
River Severn
Warwick & Napton
Stratford-on-Avon
R. Nene
Northampton
Wellingborough
Gloucester
Oxford Canal
Banbury
Grand
Junction
Canal
Oxford
River
Thames
Kennet & Avon Navigation
Reading
London

Toby of the White City

The Boat Dog's Story

1

Enuff's Enuff

"I'm not 'aving that there dog on this 'ere boat."

"Oh, be a sport, Rose", Betty pleaded to her big sister from the canal towpath. "It's freezing. Put the plank across, and let the poor little chap come aboard."

"No. We're s'posed to be working this 'ere boat to win the war, not running a travelling circus. Enuff's Enuff." Enough's enough - Rose's favourite saying.

The dog, sensing he wasn't wanted, shivered, clinging closer to Betty's old winter coat. Betty put on her sweetest little sister voice and wheedled: " 'e won't make no mess, Rose."

Rose sighed, raising her eyes to the leaden February sky. "That's just what you said about all them other pets." She stopped polishing the boat brasses for a moment and rested her arms on the cabin top. Though the late winter afternoon was raw and cold, her face in her homely knitted pixie hood was flushed with effort and smudged with coal dust.

"Who does the cleaning on this 'ere boat? Me!"

She wafted her polishing rag towards the rabbit hutches on the foredeck. "I don't mind helping you to clean out them rabbits. Them rabbits is war work, eking out our meat ration."

She waved the rag towards the budgie in his cage and the white mouse in his run. "I don't mind Budgie and Sampson aboard, but that dog will be more work than all them others put together."

"Anyway," she resumed polishing, "you'll cop it when Dad comes home. You know what 'e told you - no more livestock."

" 'e was going to be drownded", Betty protested. Rose took no notice.

The little dog looked up at Betty with a furrowed brow as if to say, "where next?" Betty didn't know. They'd already been to her Grampy's boat, the Cylgate, but nobody was at home. She stood sulking, scuffing her boot into the slushy snow piled along the towpath. She was fed up with being stuck in the ice in Banbury basin all that first winter of the war. The ice had melted now, but the canal wasn't yet cleared all the way. "Don't know what you're polishing them brasses for", she scoffed, "we ain't going nowheres."

"Any day now, that ice breaker boat'll get right through to Coventry, then we'll all be on the move again. Our chimney chain is gonna shine the bestest on the Cut."

The chimney chain secured the chimney to the boat when they had to lower it to go under low bridges. Rose loved their chimney chain. It had belonged to Grampy Hone - Captain Alfred Hone senior, the famous Number One.

The number ones were the proud independent boatmen who owned and lived on their own canal boats. Rose and Betty's Dad was a number one. He was Grampy Hone's only son. He was known as Captain Alfred Hone Junior. All his young days, he had worked hard on his father's boats, until he saved up enough money to buy the White City from his father, and marry his boat girl sweetheart Lizzie.

Each canal boat not only had a name, but had to state on the outside of the cabin who was the owner, and where it was first registered. How proud young Alf and his new bride Lizzie had been when old Mr Tooley, the boat builder at Banbury, had painted out 'Alfred Hone Sr.' and painted in 'Alfred Hone Jr.' instead. Though none of the family had had the chance to go to school and learn to read and write, they each knew by heart what that writing said. The White City had been Mum and Dad's first home. In its tiny cabin, Rose, then Betty, had been born.

By the time war broke out in 1939, the girls had grown too big to share their parents' cabin. Dad had bought another boat from Grampy Hone for the girls to work in tow with the White City. Though Rose was only twelve, and Betty was only eight, they had learned from a very early age how to handle the White City. Now they had a boat of their very own. They named her the Rose and Betty. Rose, being the elder, was the captain. She was fiercely proud of the Rose and Bet. She buffed the chimney chain to a final glow.

Betty scowled: "Cleaning mad, you is, Rosie Hone".

Without a word, Rose gathered up her cleaning things and disappeared into the cabin.

"How would you like to be gonna be drownded?", Betty flung after her.

For answer, Rose stuck the duster out of the cabin and flicked it at her.

"Right," Betty burst into tears, "enuff's enuff. You can keep the Rose and Bet all to yourself. I'm not working it. I'm going back 'ome." Clutching the dog even closer to her skinny chest, she stomped off in her high lace boots along the slushy towpath. "Mum", she yelled to the next boat, the White City, "I'm coming home. Put the plank out."

2

The Dilon Gets an 'Andle

Little Mrs Hone poked her head out from the cabin of the White City. Her wooden spoon poised, a delicious stew-laden aroma steamed out from the warm cabin behind her. She looked down upon her younger daughter on the towpath clutching yet another small creature to her bosom, and heaved a long-suffering sigh.

"What you got now, our Betsy?"

"Mum, our Rose won't let him come aboard" she yelled back along the towpath at Rose, "and he's only a little dog."

"Little dogs grows up big!", Rosie yelled back.

"This one grows up little." Betty deliberately turned her back in Rose's direction and wheedled: "Look Mum, ain't 'e pretty!"

"Where'd you pinch him from?" Mum levelled her wooden spoon at her.

"A lady gived him to me down by the drawbridge; 'e was going to be drownded. She can't afford to feed him no more, what with the rationing and all."

"And how do you think we're gonna feed him?"

The dog shot her such a worried look she couldn't help but smile. She shook her head in despair at Bet. "Ah! You knows what the captain said."

Betty tried not to think of her Dad. She stroked the dog.

" 'e's a Jack Russell, Mum."

Mum snorted "If 'e's a Jack Russell, my name's not Lizzie Lunn."

"Who's Lizzie Lunn?"

"I used to be, before I married your Dad. That's why my mother's called Granny Lunn. And that dog used to be a Jack

Russell somewhere along the line, but he ain't now. Look at them ears, all over the place. I may be no scholard, can't read and write, but I knows a Jack Russell when I sees 'em. A Jack Russell's ears should fold tidy forward, not stick out like a pair o' lock arms."

The dog licked Betty's hand as she fondled one of his wayward ears, silvery white and soft as pussy willow.

"How old is 'e?"

"Six months, the lady said."

"Six months? Looks more like six weeks."

" 'as 'e got an 'andle?"

Mum meant a handle, a name. But as she was always saying, "It's hard to get your words right way rounded, when you can't read and write."

"Dilon, the lady called 'im."

"What's a Dilon, Mum?"

"The runt of the litter, nothing but trouble."

" 'e's not having an 'andle like that." Betty clutched him protectively to her bosom. "'E's gonna be something famous."

" 'e'll never be nothing famous, not with them ears." As if to show how he would, the dog struggled to sit upright in Bet's arms, ears pricked, eyes bright and alert.

Mum laughed. " 'e's the spitting image of your Dad's Toby mug, what he shaves with."

Betty gazed deep into his glossy brown eyes. " 'Ow d'you fancy Toby as an 'andle?" The dog, fancying it was something to eat, wagged his tail. "Oh, look Mum, 'e can wag 'is tail."

"What's left of it." Mum eyed the little stump with pity. "Why they have to dock 'em like that is beyond my comprehension."

"Can I keep him, Mum?" Betty pleaded.

But Mum could see trouble approaching along the distant towpath. "You'll have to ask the captain."

3

Toby Walks the Plank

Dad strode, whistling, along the towpath, in great good humour. "Good news, Mr Rolt", he called to the captain of Cressy as he walked past. "The ice boat's cut right through to Coventry. We'll be casting off first thing in the morning."

"Even better news, Alf", Mr Rolt told him, "our troops have rescued 300 British prisoners of war off a German boat in Norway. Just heard it on the wireless." He ducked back into the smart galley of his houseboat to hear more.

Mr Rolt was a clever educated gentleman. Though Dad and Grampy Hone couldn't read or write, the three boat owners had been moored close to each other all through that terrible first winter of the war and become good friends. Dad was pleased about the prisoners, but Norway meant nothing to him. He'd never been taught to read a map. The Cut was his world, and the Cut was free from ice at last. His boats could travel again.

"Lizzie! Girls! Good news." He bounded up the plank of the White City Mum had put out for him. He whipped a piece of paper from his weskit pocket and presented it to her.

Mum clutched it to her old coat as if it were a big white five pound note. She couldn't read a word of it, but she knew it was an order - the first they'd had for weeks. The White City and the Rose and Bet were to fetch two cargoes of coal from the mines in the Midlands and deliver them down to the Co-op Wharf at Banbury. She put the order away safely in the ticket drawer. There was a lot to do if they were to cast off early in the morning.

"I'll get the supper straight away", she said. "The stew is just about ready."

"At last I can be a boatman again", Dad rejoiced to the world at large.

All that snowy winter of 1940, Dad and his boat horse Bob had been delivering milk for the Co-op in Banbury. "I'm fed up with being a milkman."

"At least Bob had some exercise, Dad", Rose piped up from the bottom of the plank where she and Betty were standing.

Dad suddenly noticed the dog in Betty's arms. His face hardened. "What did I tell yer, our Betsy?"

" 'is name's Toby, Dad."

"I don't care if he's Timbuktu."

"He was going to be drownded, Dad."

"No more livestock!"

"How would you like to be gonna be drownded, Dad?"

"I want no cheek from you, my gal. We got a war to win tomorrow. That dog would be nothing but a nuisance. Take him back."

Mum put in tactfully: "Them sort of dogs is very good at rattin', Alf."

"And gettin' stuck down rabbit holes, and holding up the boats. We're 'aving none of that lark."

Toby, not enjoying Bet's tears plopping on his nose, struggled up in her arms, begging to be put down.

"Oh look, Alf," Mum pleaded, "he's begging you to let him stop."

"Lizzie, this is no time to be messing around with a dog. What if we're invasioned?"

"Invasioned?" Mum drew herself up to her full five feet. " 'Itler wouldn't dare."

"There's only the Ditch, remember, between us and them nasties." Dad always referred to the sea as the Ditch, and the Nazis as 'them nasties'.

"A boat dog might come in 'andy, Alf - see 'em orff. Remember Nelson." Nelson was Grampy Hone's big black Labrador. He'd been dead for years, but he was still a legend on the Cut for saving many a dangerous situation.

Toby, sensing his fate was in the balance, looked soulfully

at Dad. Dad scowled at him. "You can stop if you can walk that plank."

"Oh Alf, that's a bit steep."

"Lizzie, if he can't walk that plank, 'e's no good as a boat dog.

Betty set him on the wet plank. He just clung there. Dad shook his head. "He'll never make it, legs too short."

The White City, being empty of cargo, sat high on the water, so the plank up from the towpath to the high stern was quite steep. The girls could mount it in two bounds, but to a little dog it was a slippery slope soaring into the unknown. He clung a moment, sniffing the wet worn grain. Ancient smells of coal, tar, oil, held him. He was about to venture higher, when the sharp whiff of a rat in the verge behind him sent him scampering off after it.

"Hopeless." Dad shooed Betty away. "Take him back. We've a lot to get ready if we're to cast off before dawn in the morning. It'll be time for the blackout before we've finished."

Mum, feeling she'd done all she could, ducked into the cabin with her wooden spoon to give the stew one last stir.

Betty scooped up Toby, glaring into his astonished eyes as she hurried back.

"Toby, you've got to walk that plank." He licked her nose. "Listen, it's a matter of life or death. Watch, Dad, he can do it." She plonked him higher up the plank.

Mum poked her head out of the cabin to watch. The most glorious scent of all wafted down to Toby from her wooden spoon. Food! Up the plank he panted. Up the plank he scrambled. Up the plank, he ... plop, hit the deck. He looked so surprised to find himself at Mum's feet. Even Dad couldn't help laughing.

"That's one way o' doing it."

"He's walked the plank! He's walked the plank!" Betty clapped and capered along the towpath.

" 'appy landings, Toby", Mum said kindly, ruffling his funny ears. "Welcome to the White City."

ONE
BURY
WH
CITY

4

Captain's Quarters

Late that night, Toby was curled up in Betty's doll's bath on the cabin floor of the White City. He was peeping, wide eyed, over the edge, watching Dad's strange antics.

Dad was shaving. He always shaved last thing at night. He liked to cast off each morning at the crack of dawn. Usually, with Mum tucked away in the cross bed, he had plenty of room to spread his shaving tackle on the side bed. Tonight, with Betty on the side bed and Toby under his feet, he felt cramped and irritable.

"Why must we have him in our cabin?"

"I told ya," Mum's long-suffering voice came from the hump of bedclothes Toby could see between the half-drawn bed curtains. "Rose's took enough on board captainin' the Rose and Bet. She can't cope with the dog as well. You said Betty was to be 'sponsible for him, so 'ere she is, right next to 'im. Buy 'em a boat all to 'emselves, and still they 'as to come back home!"

Betty sniffed miserably. She hadn't really meant it when she told Rose she was going back home. She hated being back in her parents' cabin. The side bed was alright when she was only little, and knew no difference. Now she was a big girl of eight. She longed for her usual comfortable berth beside Rose in the wide cross-bed of their own cabin.

" 'urry up and finish, Alf". Mum yawned. "Then you can turn the lamp out."

Toby eyed Dad warily as he lovingly dried his cut-throat razor. Dad had only two personal belongings: his best windlass for opening the locks, and his dearly cherished shaving tackle. It was his only windlass, made of special light steel and given to him when he was 14, but it was always known as his 'best'. He carried it over his shoulder, tucked under his coat during the day. At night he stowed it safely away in the monkey 'ole. His shaving tackle always lived up on the shelf with Mum's precious 'hornamentals'. Nobody was allowed to touch either of them. He turned out the lamp, opened the hatch and emptied his shaving water overboard.

" 'night, Dad" Rose called wistfully from the cabin of the Rose and Bet, now breasted up alongside.

"Go to sleep. We got a war to win in the mornin'."

Mum's candle beyond the bed curtain gave just enough light for him to see his way back. Even so, he nearly tripped headlong over Toby. He glared at the little dog.

"You be'ave yourself." Toby shrank down in his bath. "We don't want no messes, no noises. We wants a good night's sleep."

Before Mum blew out the candle, she checked that all the gas masks were there on the shelf behind her.

"Oh, chuck 'em all in the Cut", Dad growled, rocking the boat as he settled into bed. "We've 'ad them maskies on, off, on, off every time the sirens wented, and we 'aven't 'ad no air raids yet.

"Yer never knows", Mum said as she snuffed out the candle and snuggled down beside him.

All was quiet at last.

Rose, alone in the cabin of the Rose and Bet, felt utterly lost without Bet. She didn't feel she could cope with Toby, but she'd always, without question, taken care of her little sister. Though they were always squabbling, they loved each other very dearly and had never slept apart.

Betty, equally miserable without her big sister, snuffled her cuggy, the soft blanket she'd had as a comforter ever since she was a baby. She'd grown out of needing it before the war. Though she was now skilled enough to handle a 72 foot narrow boat, she hated the scary talk of the war and the awful waily wail of the air raid sirens that turned her stomach over. She needed her cuggy now more than ever.

Toby, in his doll's bath, felt lost and lonesome too. It was the first night he'd slept away from his old mother. He missed her doggy smell, her comforting warm, furry coat. It was strange in this place. The floor beneath him wouldn't keep still. He whimpered.

"Shut up", Dad growled into the pillow, "or I'll chuck you in the Cut."

Betty, thinking he meant it, burst into tears.

"Don't you start, or I'll chuck you in the Cut an' all!

Toby whimpered and whimpered. Betty boohooed.

"He don't mean it," Mum soothed, "that's just what he used to say to you when you was a baby and cried all night, but you're still here."

Toby whined and whined. Dad groaned. Toby howled and howled.

"I don't like him when 'e 'owls, Mum", Betty said.

"You took him on", Mum said wearily, "you must do something about it."

Betty had already done her best, sacrificing her doll's bath for his bed. It was a large oval tin bath, pretty painted with ducks and bull rushes. It had cost her a whole silver sixpence from the 'Threepenny and Sixpenny Store' before the war.

Still, he howled. She put out a hand to comfort him in the darkness. He was shivering all over.

"Try chucking a clorth over him," Mum suggested.

All Betty had was her precious cuggy. She took one last longing snuffle at it. Then laid it lightly over him. He sniffed, scratched, and scrabbled about under it for a while. Then all was still.

"Peace at last", mumbled Dad.

But Mum knew that without her cuggy and without Rose, Betty wouldn't sleep. Without a good sleep, she wouldn't have her wits about her to help to get the boats underway in the morning.

As soon as Dad began to snore, she whispered: "Go back to your own bed. I'll look after Toby."

As Betty stepped lightly over on to the freezing cold deck of the Rose and Bet, she felt a pang of guilt at deserting Toby. Still, she comforted herself as she thankfully nestled into her own berth beside Rose.

"I done me best."

Unbeknown to Betty, she had done the best. Toby was born in a tin bath, just like her doll's bath, but much bigger. One by one, his brothers and sisters had been sold off until he had his soft, furry mother all to himself. Betty's soft knitted cuggy was the next best thing.

On the still dark water, the White City rocked gently at her moorings. In his little bath, Toby's tiny muffled snores rose and fell in rhythm with her.

5

Toby's First Trip

Early next morning, Toby sat upright in his bath, trembling with fear. His whole world was on the move. Towing the shadowy black bows of the Rose and Bet closely in its wake, he was on the cabin top of the White City.

Mum was standing close beside him. She could just make out the pale ring of light ahead cast from Dad's shaded lantern as he trudged along the towpath beside Bob in the darkness. Boat people are said to have cats' eyes. They're so used to working in the dark.

Toby could see in the dark, too. On that cold, dank early morning in February 1940, his pupils widened to take in every glimmer of lightness. He saw the tiny sparks struck by Bob's iron shoes on the stony towpath. The faint glow from the broken ice and snow piled up all along the banks, the jagged channel of glinting black water freed by the ice boat several days before. He cowered, trembling as dark shades of wharves and warehouses loomed towards him and slid past.

"Tenches Mill, and Palmers Coal". Mum stroked him as she calmly reeled off the names of the familiar wharves and warehouses as they steered past. "Dalbey's Wood and Clarks's Flour." She held the big wooden tiller in one hand and comforted him with the other. Every time he started up in fear, she steadied him. She didn't want him falling in panic into the icy black water; 'taking a look', as they called it.

He nearly jumped out of his skin as shards of ice cracked off like pistol shots as the boat rippled past. "Nothing to be afraid of", she told him quietly, hoping he'd soon learn to trust her and settle down in his bath beside her.

Rose, behind in the darkness, at the tiller of the Rose and

Bet, could just pick out beyond the long dark mass of her own boat, the long pale horse tail flowing down the rudder of the White City. How she envied Mum that white tail. It'd belonged to Banjo, Grampy Lunn's old horse. Boat people believed that the spirit of a good, faithful horse lived on in its tail after death, and brought good luck.

Rose shuddered deeply with the cold. Her feet were freezing. She stamped her boots on the top step. She stood penned in the slide 'ole, with the catch doors closed behind her. Normally, with the boats travelling empty, she needn't steer. Like a mother duck, where the White City led, the closely tied Rose and Bet would automatically follow. But after all these weeks, with nobody using the Cut, she told Betty, "You never knows."

In the lamp lit cabin immediately below, Betty shovelled coal on the fire.

"I'll soon 'ave this range blazing, Rose, get your bottom half toasted."

Toby, getting used to the strange motion of the White City, settled down with a sigh and let Mum's running commentary wash over him.

"You know what makes the world go round, Toby? Coal."

The chimney beside him was getting pleasantly warm as the smoke from the cosy range below drifted out of the top. "Chimlies, chimlies, the 'ole world over. Cabins and castles, foundries and factories."

On the bank ahead, hundreds of shaded lanterns and bicycle lamps came weaving and bobbing towards them.

"Well, must be six o'clock", Mum said. "The night shift's coming out of the aluminium works factory. Soon, the next shift will take over, and another after that. The factories have to be kept going night and day, making metal for planes and munitions for our lads to fight the war."

Toby couldn't understand a word she was saying, but her kind, motherly voice was very reassuring.

Mum was enjoying his company, even though he was only a little dog. Though the rest of the family were all within hailing distance, they were not close enough to chat. Mum loved to chat. She had no other entertainment. She often had to endure long, lonely stretches of steering without a word to anyone, whereas the girls had each other, and Dad had Bob.

"Steady, old chap." It was the second time Bob had nearly stumbled into the Cut. He knew every inch of the ground, even in the dark. But after weeks of bad weather, the bank had broken away in places.

Toby studied Mum's face intently. A pale light shone on it. He peeped over the edge of his bath to see where it was coming from. Beyond the black silhouette of a lift bridge ahead, a long low band of daylight silvered along the dusky horizon. Gradually, it spread up the sky until he could see Mum's face quite clearly. He sat up and took notice. Soon he could see right along the hold to the mast of the White City. And then the tow rope stretching across to Bob's swingletree. And then the whole wintry landscape through which Bob was towing them.

Bob and the Hone family had worked this route for years. He wore out a lot of shoes as mile after mile, day after day, year after year, he drew the two empty boats from Banbury to the mine "down the north" and the two heavily laden boats of coal back home again to Banbury. Dad always led Bob by the head. In that way they kept each other going at a steady two miles an hour. The complete trip from Banbury to Baddesley and back took about a week, "providing we 'as a good road", Dad called it. One hundred and twenty four miles altogether. Dad had never seen a map of it. He needed no map. He knew every lock, bridge, tree, farm, feature the winding canal revealed on the varying landscape.

Bob's map was the terrain under his feet. The scrunchy track of the towpath. The smooth worn brick sets at each lock side. The hollow iron echo of each horse bridge and the homely cobbles of each familiar stable along the way.

From that very first trip, Toby too began to make his own map. Scents and sounds of people and places, especially at the many locks the family gathered as a team to operate. At his first lock, he had leapt in terror onto the lock side. To and fro, he raced, hackles up, growling and yapping fiercely at the churning monster of water heaving the White City up to the next level.

"It's only a lock, you daft 'aporth", Mum had laughed.

By the end of his first day, many locks later, he had learned to "Shut up", "Sit!" and watch the procedure with a wary interest from the lock side.

By the end of his second day, he'd discovered double locks and how much quicker it was for two boats to be worked through at the same time instead of wasting time waiting for each other.

By the end of his third day, he'd learnt to be brave and "Stay" beside Mum on the cabin top and "Wait" their turn at the busier locks down the north, and even more patiently in the queue of boats, waiting their turn to be loaded with coal from the railway trucks at the mine beyond Atherstone. Most important of all in Toby's map were the people who gave him something to eat or drink. The families and lock keepers who'd given him a titbit or a drink of fresh milk. Granny and Grampy Lunn, Mum's Mum and Dad, who'd given him fish and chips and made a great fuss of him in their retirement house on the bank at Atherstone. He noted too all those who gave him a kind word and a friendly pat. Those who had offered to fill the water cans for Mum and the girls, or chatted, or passed on the news of the war to Dad.

"The German U-boats are going to sink every ship in the Channel from now on, Alf", Mr Veater, the toll officer at Sutton Stop, told Dad on their way home.

Dad was disgusted. "Even those not in the war?"

Mr Veater nodded. Toby was watching Mr Veater's every movement as he measured the depth of the White City in the stop lock, and worked out how much money he would have to charge Banbury Co-op for using the canal.

"They want to stop neutral ships bringing us vital food and materials. They're going to starve us into surrender."

Mum sighed: "It's already a struggle to make the rations go round. Wonder what they'll ration next?"

"Coal", Mr Veater told them. "The country needs all the coal it can get to keep the factories going. You're carrying a valuable cargo here, Alf. Watch where you moor tonight. There's a lot of pilfering going on. Make sure this dog of yours keeps his ears open."

In the middle of that night, Toby's whiskers twitched. He could sense movement outside. He raised his head from his bath in the cabin of the White City and pricked his ears. Stealthy footsteps were creeping past the boat. He roused Dad with a soft growl. They both listened intently. Toby felt the boat rock slightly. He heard the faint chink of a bucket handle. Somebody had boarded the boats.

Quietly, Dad opened the cabin door. Out shot Toby, barking furiously. Dad smiled as he heard a man's muffled curse, the clang and clatter of a falling bucket and rapid footsteps racing away with Toby in noisy pursuit. Toby's distant barking suddenly deepened and echoed. He'd chased the thief right through a tunnel and up a steep bank of trees. He waited, panting and listening up at the top. Making sure the man had fled, he then trotted back home to the White City, very pleased with himself.

In the morning, they found the bucket in the grassy verge with several lumps of best coal strewn along the bank. They also discovered a hessian sack half stuffed with hay flung on the fore deck of the Rose and Bet.

"The cheek of it," Betty told everybody indignantly on

their way home, "he was going to pinch my rabbits too."

Mom was delighted with the nearly new galvanised bucket.

"Just what I need to carry the water for my washing tub."

Bob was delighted with the extra hay.

Rose was delighted with the hessian sack.

"Just what I need to protect my paintwork." She hung it on the side as they moored at Banbury to be unloaded at the end of their trip.

And Betty was delighted with Toby. He'll be as famous as Grampy's Nelson one day, Dad. "Told yer he'd make a good boat dog."

"Boat dog", Dad scoffed, leading old trooper Bob off to the stables for a well-earned rest. "He's only done one trip!"

6

Boat Dog

By the time the catkins were out and on the bank, Toby had done several trips. He'd grown out of Betty's doll's bath. He no longer slept in the stuffy cabin. He preferred to sleep outside on an old sack in the hatches when the boats were empty, and on an old tarpaulin, or 'flat' as they called it, on the coal when the boats were loaded. Even in his sleep, he was always on guard. Just a low growl was enough to scarper a thief or scamper a rat. He always looked upon the White City as his boat.

When Betty's rabbits were evacuated to the safety of Granny Lunn's back yard on the bank at Atherstone, Rose invited him to move back onto the Rose and Bet. But when Betty tried to carry him aboard, his little legs fought like pistons. He leapt for the towpath and shot back home. He no longer walked the plank. Light as a bird, he hopped from path to plank to tiller to cabin top, and there he would gather himself into the tiniest space to sit down. "Squatting on a sixpence", Mum called it. He had a wonderful view from his perch on the cabin top.

As March blew into April, "Stay!" was the hardest command Toby had to learn to obey. "Stay!" Quivering with self-control, he had to just "Sit there!" while all along the Cut mallard ducks taunted him, tossing water from their shot-silk heads flaunting at him their purple under-feathers. "Stay!" Mother ducks deliberately marshalled their tempting little fluffy ducklings right under his nose. "Stay!" Farm dogs barked insults at him as they rounded up cows for milking from the water meadows. Swifts swooped within inches of his head, cockerels crowed and mother sheep stamped at him, "Stay!", guarding their timid little lambs on the bank. He loved the life.

Though they always worked the same route, every trip was different. Full of constant interest, variety and human company for a little lively, friendly dog. Wind, sun, rain, fog; Toby took them all on board. He soon became a great help in fog. Only one boat at a time could fit through the narrow bridge-'oles; there was always the danger of colliding. Toby sensed an oncoming boat long before the putt-putt-putt-putt-putt of its engine came into Dad's earshot. He'd drum his little round front paws on the cabin top, warning Mum with short excited yelps.

Mum would give three loud blasts on a battered old bugle Grampy Hone had given them. The engine boat would have to be held back to allow the horse drawn boats through first, and how the crew would smile after Mum's loud fanfare to see only a little dog with funny ears looking down his nose at them through the mist.

He soon found his boat-legs. He'd inspect the White City umpteen times a day, patrolling the low gunwales within inches of quacking ducks or trip-trotting along the top planks within a claw's width of the deep drop into the empty hold.

When Betty wasn't taking her turn at steering, she would walk him along the tow path. After he'd 'scorted orf' after rabbits a few times, she kept him on a rope. He trotted miles in the wake of Dad and Bob. Full of his own importance, he'd weave from side to side of the path, pretending to be a sheepdog, driving them to market.

Mum always made sure that Dad had thick leather soles to his boots. "Leather lets feets breathe", she always said. Every print those boots made, breathed 'Dad' to the myriad nerve endings in Toby's clever nose. If ever he lost his bearings, he had only to sniff the air for the weedy, watery direction of the Cut. Once back on the towpath, he could easily sniff out Dad's prints. His fine nose would tell him how recently Dad had walked there, which direction he was travelling and even if he was angry with Toby for 'scorting orf'. He never 'scorted orf' for more than one night, and only when the boats were empty. If they had to moor out from the bank, Mum would always leave the plank out for him.

"It's 'ere", Dad would announce first thing next morning. There Toby would be, flat out on his sack in the hatches, covered in mud with a dead rabbit, or on more than one guilty occasion, somebody's plump chicken beside him.

"Come for your bed and breakfast, have yer?"

Whimpering with delight, Toby would hurl himself into Dad's arms, licking him all over like a long lost friend. Dad would never let on that he was pleased. "Daft 'aporth", was all he'd say.

"Bossy boots", Mr Veater always called Toby.

Whenever the toll officer measured the boats in the stop lock, Toby would stand on his hind legs in the hatches, pause on the edge of the boat, watching closely as Mr Veater put his gauging stick into the water beside the boat. He'd peer intently as Mr Veater read it off, making sure he got it right. Mr Veater had measured the Hone's boats so often, he knew how many inches of dry side or free board, as they called it, the White City showed when empty; he could work out how much coal she was carrying. When he crossed the lock to measure the other side, Toby would shoot across the deck to supervise that side too.

The Hone family, with their painted boats and old boat horse Bob, had been a familiar sight for years along the Cut. Now, Toby was an accepted and valued member of the crew. But Dad made it quite clear: "If ever Toby missed the boat, there'd be no holding up the boats to look for him. We 'as a war to win. We 'as to battle on."

In that lovely spring of 1940, it was still difficult to believe there was a war. From time to time, Toby yapped as a column of soldiers route-marched along a canalside road or a convoy of armoured cars and army lorries gingerly eased their way, one at a time, over a narrow old hump-backed canal bridge. He was used to the noisy aircraft whizzing "out London Way", as Mum called it, but as long as his beloved White City kept rippling on at a steady two miles an hour, he was happy to battle on in peace.

As April cuckooed into May, snippets of news trickled through of German raids on British airfields, of sinkings at sea, and battles " 'cross the ditch". But as May trundled into June with the great cart horses pulling the hay carts loaded to their limits, the trickle of news became a spate of garbled disasters.

" 'Itler's pinched Denmark."

"Nazi parachutists have took Norway."

" 'Olland's gone."

"Belgie's gone."

"Jerrys are marching into Paris."

"England next, 'Itler says."

"That settles it, Lizzie", Dad decided grimly, "I'm not wearing that gas maskey no more. I can't see nothing in that steamed up rubber maskey. When 'Itler lands 'ere, I wants to see 'xactly whom I'm up against."

Two weeks later, loaded with coal, the boats were moored in the only patch of shade at Napton top lock. There had been no rain for weeks. They were waiting for two boats to come from the Banbury direction to share the locks, like people having to use the same bath of water to conserve precious water because the canal was so low.

The girls sat on the cabin top of the White City with Toby flopped out between them. They were making him a daisy chain and serenading him with a little song they'd made up.

"Oh where, oh where, has our little dog gone? Oh where, oh where, can he be? With his tail docked short and his ears all wrong, oh where, oh where, is he?"

Toby flicked the fly from his eyebrow to show he was still listening. Budgie and Samson were snoozing on the cabin top of the Rose and Bet. Bob, released from the tow rope, was idly cropping the dusty verge. Mum and Dad were sitting on the grass beside the White City having a mug of tea. The whole countryside was buzzing and shimmering in the blazing June heat. Not another sign of life was in sight.

"I reckon the 'ole country's gone to war and left us in the dumps."

Dad mopped his sweltering brow with his big red neckerchief. Mum sighed.

"I can't believe them Nasties is winning the war, Alf. I wish I was edicated. I'd give anythink to open one of they newspapers and read all the goings on for myself. If Mr Rolt was still moored alongside us, we could ask him the goings on. Oh yes, Mr Rolt was proper edicated. 'E were writing a real book."

"He's still writing his book?" Rose piped up. "Mrs Skinner seed him down at Tooley's boatyard the other day. Cressy's moored down Hungerford way now." She had no idea where Hungerford was, but like her mother, she loved to chat.

"He's got a motorbike, says it takes less petrol ration than his old Alvis car. Mrs Skinner was buying one of them batteries, Dad. Mr Skinner's fixed one of them newfangled wireless sets in her monkey 'ole on the Friendship so theys can keep up with the war.

"Can we have a newfangled wireless in our monkey 'ole, Dad?" Betty wheedled.

"No. Them 'cumulator batteries cost a fortune. Sixpence a swap. It's alright for Joe and Rose Skinner, they ain't got no children, only their old mule, Dolly. We've got you and your menagerie."

"Toby's not menagerie." Betty crowned his ears with a daisy chain. "Toby's king of the Cut."

Toby, used to Betty's titivations, raised one eyebrow to his crown and carried on snoozing.

"Whatever's that, Dad?"

Rose pointed to a strange round building that had cropped up like a mushroom along the bank.

"A pillbox."

"What for?"

"Jerry parachuters."

Betty stared at it, wide eyed. Whatever did they take all them pills for?"

"Not Beechams pills, you daft 'aporth" Mum laughed.

"What's it doing next to our Cut, Dad?" Rose asked.

"This 'ere Cut's the heart of old England, gal. If 'Itler captures the heart of old England, he'll win the war."

"You won't let him though, will you Dad?"

Rose had complete faith in her Number One Dad. Dad drained his mug of tea and shook his head.

"When the belly of that Jerry plane opens and all them Nasties comes floating down, I shall be in that pillbox picking them orf."

"With pills, Dad?"

Betty still didn't understand. "Cartridges, gal, cartridges."

"You'll have a job with your old .410, Alf,"

"Lizzie, I've had many a pigeon with that old .410."

"I know, but if you keep stopping to load up with them old BB cartridges, and pull back both 'ammers...."

Betty, hating all this talk about guns and Nasties, flung her arms round Toby.

"You'll see him orf, won't you, Toby?"

Toby, hearing "see him orf", shot to his feet, his daisy crown awry. Drumming his paws on the cabin top, he yelped with delight. He could hear a boat engine coming, at last. Dad shot to his feet.

"I know that old Petter hengine."

"Hurray." The girls scrambled down off the cabin top. "It's the Littlemores."

The Littlemores, another boat family with children, had only recently converted from a horse drawn to an engine boat. Now, the children of both families were in for a treat, the chance to run about on the bank and play together with Toby. He was soon leading them all a merry chase round and round and in and out the pillbox, while the grown-ups chatted, helping each other to work the four boats through the lock.

Late the next evening, Dad plodded heavy-hearted towards his boats. Once again, they were moored at their home-town, Banbury. Their holds swept clean of coal, paintwork washed, brasses polished, and rations stowed for the coming week.

Mum and the girls were sitting in the hatches of the White City. Mum was busy with her crochet and Rose was teaching Betty to crochet. Toby, standing lookout on the cabin top, wagged his whole body to welcome Dad. "Bad news", Dad announced gravely, "they've dumped us in the Ditch."

"Who's dumped us in the Ditch?"

"All them countries what begged us to help 'em fight the Nasties. Czechs, Poles, Belgies, Dutch, Frenchies, what have yer, all gived in. Left us to it. Dumped us in the Ditch."

"Who told yer?"

"Tooleys' wireless down at the boatyard. Nine o'clock news. These past weeks, our poor chaps have been trapped on a beach called Dunkirk. Trapped between Jerry and the Ditch. Jerry planes and guns have been pounding 'em to death. Our Navy went to rescue 'em, but them big ships couldn't get near enough without getting stemmed up. Lots of little boats, pleasure boats, cockle boats, Number Ones, what have yer, have been nipping over from England, fishing 'em off."

"Can we go, Dad?" Rose begged.

"No, there's no towpath cross't the Ditch, gal. Even if we was engine boats, we aren't built for navigation in the 'igh seas."

Mum agreed. "The waves would come right up over the cratch and drown the lot of us."

"There must be something we can do."

Rose studied the boats so perfectly reflected on the sunset water.

"All we can do," Dad said with a glint of battle in his eye, "is keep these 'ere boats a'working. Gas, 'lectric, steam - all comes from coal. Without the coal, the 'ole nation's had it."

"But what if there's one poor soldier still left, Dad?"

"Too late, Rose, them Nasties is swarming all over now."

Mum said quietly. "It's all up to us from now on."

Betty didn't feel up to anything. Her face crumpled into tears.

"Rose!"

Rose drew her close, struggling to contain her own fears.

"Pluck up!" Dad rallied them all. "We've a sound pair o' boats and a good boat horse."

Toby, on the cabin top, nudged him with his cold wet nose. "Oh yes, and a jolly good boat dog."

He ruffled Toby's ears. "We can take it, eh Toby?"

Toby licked him eagerly. Whatever *it* was, he was game.

7

Toby Makes an Important Discovery

Very early the next morning, Toby trotted along as usual with Dad and Rose to fetch Bob from the stables. Snuffling with excitement through the lush, dewy verge, he scented a vole ahead and chased after it.

Rose loved the Cut at this fresh hour of the morning. She couldn't bear to think of those poor soldiers trapped on the other side of the Ditch when her own world was aglow with the warmth of the rising sun. Only the sleepy chirrup of a bird and the plop of the vole escaping from Toby, broke the magic stillness. A thin rosy pink mist drifted over the water. The canal, like a ribbon of gold, threaded itself to the hazy horizon.

"The Cut looks as though it goes on forever and ever, don't it, Dad?"

Dad swelled with pride. "You can get anywheres from here, girl."

Rose, equally proud of her beloved Cut, walked tall in her faded boat bonnet, carefully carrying Bob's breakfast in the 'nosten'.

Bob's nose tin, or nosten as they called it, was pretty painted with full blown canal roses and "WHITE CITY" painted on it. It fastened with a strap to Bob's harness. They could use it like a nose bag for him to feed on the trip, or as a feeding bowl in the stable. This morning, Dad had mixed for him his favourite mash as a treat.

"He's battling to win the war, same as the rest of us."

The stables belonged to a pub called the Leathern Bottle. For many years, Grampy Hone had paid the landlord five shillings a week to keep two standings always clean and ready for his 'hanimals'. This was quite a lot of money when there were plenty of other stables charging only fourpence a night. But it meant that, however late at night the Hone boats tied up at Banbury, there was always a clean, dry, stable waiting for their horses. This morning, the stables seemed so gloomy and deserted after the bright sunlight outside.

Rose could just recall the days before the war, when every stable had had a horse, and the yard would have been full of children helping their dads with their horses. This morning, not even the Grantham's old cob, nor the Skinner's mule Dolly, was there.

Rose sighed. "Bob's got the stable all to hisself again, Dad." She wedged the nosten of mash in the manger. Toby automatically hopped up and began tucking in.

There were few special pet foods in those days, and none the boat people could afford. Like most working dogs, Toby had to exist most of the time on what he could catch or scavenge. Bob was very easy going, and Toby was only a small dog. He soon had his fill. He set off on his usual ritual, a drink from the pump through in the pub yard and a chase of the pub cat.

He was a fierce, wicked old tomcat called One Eyed 'Itler. Out the yard he streaked, with Toby yapping after him, down the alley into Factory Street, round the knackers yard, round the boat yard, in the yard again, round the pump, up the beer casks up to the pub roof, and there Toby left him swinging on the pub sign, spitting and caterwauling. Very pleased with himself, he trotted back to the stable and sat panting, supervising Rose grooming Bob.

Rose had loved brushing out Bob's glossy brown coat and combing out his long, creamy tail. She took great care that every little strap of harness lay flat and comfortable for the long day's haul ahead. Last of all, she put on his new ear caps. She was so proud of those ear caps. They were the first pair she had made all by herself. Mum had shown her the traditional boat horse pattern. They fitted neatly over his ears to keep out the midges that pestered him along the towpath. They had soft silky tassels too, for Bob to whisk away the flies as he plodded along. She led him out into the yard.

"How's that then, Dad?"

Bob, with his clean ear caps, coloured trace bobbins and polished horse brasses, looked every inch a champion boat horse.

Toby made his last minute check of the rest of the stables. They all smelled of the usual dung, hay, coal - except the far one. He stiffened; something foreign in there. Hackles up, he crept in. Out he shot, nearly sending Bob and Dad flying across the cobbled yard.

"Out of it", Dad growled at him.

There was something in that stable Dad should know about. Toby wasn't going to let him lead Bob out of that yard until he looked. He yapped, he pranced, he fussed in and out of Bob's hooves.

"Out of it!" Dad bellowed at him.

Out of the dark stable stumbled a soldier, filthy, unkempt and befuddled with sleep.

"Blimey, mate", Dad gaped, "who are you?"

"Dar... Darby, Pri... Private number 526"; the mumbled numbers trailed away.

He looked at Dad in a daze.

"English?"

"Course we'm English."

The soldier couldn't believe his eyes. He glanced from Bob's ear caps to Rose's bonnet to Dad's bright neckerchief.

"Boatman?"

Dad drew himself up very proud in his hobnail boots.

"Captain Alfred Hone Junior of the White City and the Rose and Betty."

The soldier flung his arms round Dad, tears running down into his dirty whiskers. "I'm back to the Cut, the beautiful Cut."

"Ooh", Dad eased him away. "Where have you been, soldier?"

Dad's eyes narrowed. "You a deserter?"

"I'm a survivor, mate." He still couldn't believe it. Laughing and sobbing with amazement, he slumped back against the stable door, "A bloody survivor", and subsided slowly to the cobbles.

"From Dunkirk?" Rose asked, wide eyed.

He nodded weakly.

Dad stared in utter amazement. "How did you fetch yourself back here?"

The soldier painfully recalled "We were sent back from the front, from the beach to blow up our fuel dump. Couldn't leave Jerry with all that petrol. We done it. Our little group. Load up the lot. We was cut off behind enemy lines. Took us days to get back to the beach, hiding in ditches, pig sties, what 'ave yer. Only me and the quartermaster made it back to Dunkirk. Quart copped it as we was wading out to the boat. I tried to hold on to him .... out of me depth. Gets back to Blighty. There's thousands of us - Brits, Poles, French, Dutch. Goodness knows where they'll billet all of us. They says to me: "Clean yourself up. Here's your travel warrant. Go home on leave and await further orders."

"Oi can't read no travel warrants. My 'ome's the Cut. Couldn't stop to clean up. This lorry driver was just orf. 'Put me down by the Cut, mate', I says, 'any Cut. I can get home from there' ."

Rose nodded. "You can get anywheres from here."

Toby, who'd been smelling the soldier all over, began licking his boots. The soldier smiled grimly.

"He can taste the salt." His hand shook as he stretched to stroke the bright eyed little dog.

"That seaside were no picnic, doggy. No picnic."

"If he 'adn't flushed yer out, we'd be gone by now", Dad told him, "we'll 'ave to get moving, Soldier, else they'll be calling you back to the front before you've even been 'ome on

leave. Which Cut you from? He closed his eyes as if to picture the most beautiful Cut in the world. "The Shroppie", he whispered.

Dad had heard of the Shroppie, the Shropshire Union Canal, but he'd never worked on it. "Uh, down the north, ain't it?"

The soldier was too exhausted to answer. His head sunk on his chest. Rose crouched beside him to prop him up.

"We'em going down the north." She looked anxiously up at her Dad as the soldier slumped against her. "I reckon he's proper wore out. Dad." She touched his rough, blood stained battle dress to make sure she wasn't dreaming. A real soldier, a brave boatman soldier. Her heart swelled with pride.

"Don't you worry no more, soldier. We'll rescue yer."

8

'Ome Sweet 'Ome

"Abe Darby of the Cain & Abel is alive and well, and coming home."

The good news spread like wildfire along the Cut. Few people who lived near the canal in those days were linked to telephone lines. Messages had to travel by the grapevine, word of mouth carried by boat, bike, horse or on foot.

Not only boatmen; wharf men and lock keepers spread the good news, but also people who worked in canalside villages. The milkman, spanking along with his pony and float, the measures jangling against the churns at the back. The postman, weaving and wobbling on his big red GPO bike, its basket on the front filled with post for those lucky people who could read and write. The farmer driving his herd to be milked, or leading his horse and waggon out into the hayfield.

Soon, every boat that chugged towards them on that glorious June morning in 1940 hailed the Hone family with a cheer. They were pleased and proud that they were bringing home one of their own, a brave boatman from Dunkirk.

"Toby found him", Mum broadcast to them all in passing.

"Watcha, Toby!"

They stuck up their thumbs to him in approval. Toby, at his customary lookout post on the cabin top, wagged his stumpy tail, pleased to be of service.

"His Mum and Dad are number ones", Mum informed everybody, "on the Shroppie, 'orse drawed. Same as us." She thumbed over her shoulder. "He's fast asleep on the Rose and Bet."

"Watcha, Rose." They all gave her the thumbs up too.

Rose, at the tiller of the Rose and Bet, beamed and blushed in her old-fashioned sun bonnet. She felt very honoured to be in charge of such an important cargo.

"A soldier of His Majesty, King George the Sixth" the lock keeper at Banbury had written on the special permit allowing "Captain Alfred Hone Junior of the White City and Rose and Betty to travel without let or hindrance."

"That means we haven't got to share the locks", Mum told Mrs Adkins, the lock keeper's wife, when they reached Cropredy, "else we'd be held up to kingdom come, and the poor soldier would never get home to his Mum and Dad."

Mrs Adkins was filling up Mum's saucepans and buckets with water from her well, so Mum could do Abe's washing.

"It's a good thing we are travelling empty", Mum told her. "I can do me washing in the 'old as we're going along. Our Bet'll take over the steering. Alf's fixed me washing line."

She showed her the terrible state of Abe's uniform and underclothes. Mrs Adkins grimaced at the blood stains. "Is he wounded?"

"No, praise be. All he needs is a good, long sleep. He's been in the thick of battle these last few weeks, and he's only a lad."

Mum should know. She'd bathed and tended him as if he were her only son. She'd put him into Dad's only spare night shirt and settled him to sleep on the cross-bed of the Rose and Bet.

"I couldn't have him in 'ere." She puffed back her hair from her flushed face, as she set the kettles and pans to boil. "He'd cook to death with this range going."

She showed Mrs Adkins the battered photograph she'd found in his uniform pocket. "That's him with his Mum and his Dad, and their boats all spruced up for the old King's Silver Jubilee."

Mrs Adkins studied it with interest. "My, look at that ropework".

Mum laughed. "The only other thing he salvaged was this."

She held up a smooth wooden peg - a boatman's fid for

making rope work. Mrs Adkins laughed.

"Oh, you can tell he's a boatman."

She studied the photo again. "His Mum and Dad look old."

"Well, he is the youngest of seven brothers. None of the others took to the boats. He was their only one, their righthand mate. How they must miss him."

Mrs Adkins handed the photo back, and Mum put it safely away with his fid in the ticket drawer.

By now, Dad and 'Lija Adkins had finished working the boats through the lock. Mrs Adkins hurried into her cottage and came out with a parting gift. Some precious soap flakes. Soap was rationed in the war, and soap flakes were very difficult to get. "For the soldier", she said simply. "For the soldier. For the soldier."

All sorts of little gifts were handed over to Betty and Mum on the White City as they travelled along. Nothing grand. A few ounces of tea or sugar, a little pat of home-made butter, a pot of homemade jam, a box of matches. All these things were rationed and getting very scarce.

Toby, wagging his tail thinking each gift was for him, usually got a titbit as well.

"For the soldier." Mrs Bloomfield, wife of the foreman at the Claydon Canal Maintenance Yard, greeted Mum with some new laid eggs from her Rhode Island Red hens.

"Like to see him?" Mum asked, as if Abe was a prize exhibit. While Toby supervised the men working the White City through the lock, the womenfolk clustered at the open slide of the Rose and Betty. Abe Darby was curled up deep asleep, his arm shielding his head as if fending off attack.

"I 'ad ever such a job with him at first", Rose confided in a low voice, her young face full of motherly concern. "He kept struggling to get past me up these steps."

"Got to blow up the dump", he says, "Got to blow up the dump!"

"I said: 'You 'aint blowing nowheres. You're safe on the Cut.' If I hadn't been wearing this old bonnet, I don't think he'd have believed me. He took one look at me bonnet, then meek as a lamb, he shuffles back to bed. He hasn't moved since Lat Mill, not even when all they noisy Spitfires came whizzing over."

"Oh, let's hope you'll hear from his Mum and Dad before he has to report back", Mrs Bloomfield said to Mum.

"Oh, there's been train loads of battle-weary soldiers passing through these last few days."

Dad and Bob were just moving off as the postman arrived at the lockside with the latest news.

"That rotten dictator, Mussolini, has declared war on us."

Betty saw all the grown-ups look at each other in dismay.

"Who's Muscle Meany, Dad?"

"A rotten dictator what sits on the fence watching the fight till he sees who's winning, then pitches in against the loser."

"Ah, he'll find out", he called back to the postman as he and Bob plodded on.

"We shall win! Then the bullies'll be scuppered."

Toby supervised from the cabin top as Mum worked hard, winding the handle of the mangle to wring out Abe's washing. She lifted the basket of clean washing up onto the plank and clambered up beside it. The washing line stretched from cabin to mast. The canal and the railway side by side curved away into the distance beyond it. She'd almost finished working her way along the plank, pegging out the washing, when the whistle of a steam train sounded behind them.

"Oh, blow that for a lark", she said, "I hope he don't puff his dirty smuts all over my clean washing."

She clutched Abe's battle dress top to her. It had taken ages to get clean. As the first carriage steamed slowly past, they saw it was packed with weary soldiers crowded against the windows. Toby yapped at them with excitement and pranced his little war dance on the cabin top. Dad stuck up his thumb to them and gave them a cheer.

A ripple of amusement spread over the tired faces. Here, with their mongrel dog, painted boats and old-fashioned boat horse was a bit of old England still plodding on. From carriage to carriage, windows were let right down on their wide leather straps. Soldiers leaned out, waving, cheering and wolf whistling.

"We're going to 'ang out the washing on the Siegfried line" Mum sang out, flaunting Abe's battle top. Strong voices picked up the popular wartime song until every carriage was singing it. Snatches of it still floated back defiantly as the last carriage clickety-clacked away, a dwindling Union Jack being vigorously waved by the guard at the back.

Toby watched it, wagging his tail till the tiny flag was out of sight when, with a deep sigh of satisfaction, he squatted back on his neat little haunches on the cabin top. Mum beamed at him. "That cheered 'em up. Toby!"

Betty, highly delighted, yelled back at Rose. "They whistled me."

"No, they didn't. They whistled me!"

Rose clapped a hand to her loud mouth, remembering her sleeping passenger. She ducked to see into the cabin. Abe was still asleep. She wondered where his Mum and Dad were, and how soon they would hear that their son was safe and coming home. There was so much she wanted to ask him about the war, and about the Cain & Abel. How she envied their smart rope work. She loved to be able to make rope work like that for the Rose and Bet. 'Ah, how long will he sleep?', she wondered.

All that long, hot summer day, Abe slept. Swifts called, ducks quacked. People chatted and paddles clattered. Waters gushed and poured and swirled. And still he slept. The boats rose lock after lock to the highest level of the Cut and floated on through miles of sun-baked meadows. Cattle up to their knees in flowers lined the banks solemnly chewing their cud and eyeing the boats lazily as they passed. Little humpy backed bridges with their old canal number plates and bright wild flowers springing from mossy crevices slid their cool dark shadows over them, and still he slept. He slept all that day, all that night, and well into the next day.

Very late in the afternoon, he awoke. A little stitched picture 'Home Sweet Home' was on the cabin wall at the foot of the bed. For a moment, he couldn't recognise where he was. Then it all came flooding back with a rush of joy and relief. He was going home, home on leave.

"You've got to report", Dad sadly informed him.

"Oh, no."

"Tonight."

"Tonight?"

Dad gave him a huge wink.

"To the Greyhound Inn, Sutton Stop, where your Mum and Dad with the Cain & Abel loaded to the gunwales with Cheshire cheeses for Coventry will be there to welcome you."

"Oh, where, oh where, has our little dog gone? Oh, where, oh where can he be? With his tail docked short and his ears all wrong. Oh, where, oh where is he?"

It was a very smart young soldier indeed that serenaded Toby at the top of his voice at the tiller of the White City late that afternoon. On the Rose and Bet closely roped behind him, Mum and the girls were joining in. Mum, determined that Abe should receive to the full his hero's welcome, had handed over the White City entirely to him and Toby on this final stretch of their trip to Sutton Stop.

Toby, sitting on the cabin top beside him, kept glancing up at Abe's straight parting and down to his clean boots, as if to make sure this singing soldier was really the same scruffy survivor he had discovered in the stable at dawn only yesterday morning.

After a very late breakfast of new laid eggs, homemade butter, homemade bread and jam, Mum had given him a haircut. He'd appreciated beyond words the luxuries of Dad's precious shaving kit, Mum's tin bath of piping hot water and his clean washed and pressed clothes and uniform.

As Bob and Dad plodded round the final bend to Sutton Stop, the full glow of a huge setting sun flashed on Bob's polished brasses, and washed over the graceful bow and painted cratch of the White City to shine on Abe, with Toby beside him at the tiller. A great cheer went up from all the crews moored along the bank, crowded on the quay and on the horse bridge, as if on cue, a flight of Spitfires and Hurricanes raced overhead. It was a tremendous welcome.

Toby, thinking it was for him, wagged his tail in excitement. Abe could see the Cain & Abel dressed overall with flags in front of the Greyhound. His old Mum and Dad were standing in the hatches, just as they were in his treasured photo. The times he'd looked at that battered photo during these last terrible months of bitter fighting, dreading he'd never see them again. Tears of joy ran down his cheeks. Bursting with happiness, he caught up the dear little boat dog beside him and held him close.

"There's no place like home, Toby. No place like home."

Toby, licking away Abe's tears, warmly agreed.

9

The Secret Grapevine

"We shall defend our island, whatever the cost may be. We shall fight on the beaches, we shall fight on the landing grounds, we shall fight in the fields and streets."

A week had passed since Abe's homecoming; a week in which brave British fighter pilots and gun crews had duelled night and day against wave after wave of German bombers, keeping at bay Hitler's threatened invasion.

Toby sat on Dad's lap in the Bull and Butcher pub at Napton, listening to the powerful man's voice coming from the big wooden wireless. Usually, he'd be sitting on Dad's lap watching the boatmen play pub games, but tonight the dominoes, darts, shove ha'penny and table skittles lay idle in the shadows. The men were gathered in the ring of lamp light round the wireless. Toby could tell by their intense listening, weather-beaten faces that he must sit very still and listen too.

"We shall never surrender! Let us brace ourselves to do our duty and so bear ourselves as a nation that in years to come, men will say 'This was their finest hour'."

Old Farmer Green turned off the wireless. A grim silence filled the homely farmhouse parlour. They all looked to Charlie, Farmer Green's son, to tell them what they must do. Charlie was in the new local defence volunteers. Charlie was Toby's friend. Whenever Toby trotted up to the cow shed or cattle pen, Charlie would always give him a drink of fresh milk or toss him a piece of cattle cake.

"That was our new Prime Minister, Mr Churchill", Charlie explained. "The Germans could land here any day now. They'll probably drop down by parachute like they did in Holland. We must fight them every inch of the way." His heart sank as he looked at their drawn, anxious faces. Almost all of the boatmen were over 70. They were worn out already from years of struggling to earn a living from the Cut. Only Alf and his little dog, Toby, had any go about them.

"We'll have a go, Charlie", Dad promised, "won't we, Toby?"

Toby looked up eagerly from Dad to Charlie. Whatever they were going at, he was game.

Charlie urged the others. "Even if you can't fight, Mr Churchill says, you must do anything you can to stop the enemy's advance. Build roadblocks. Take down or paint out any signs that may give them information."

"First thing tomorrow, son." Farmer Green butted in. "We must take down our old pub sign over the door. If Jerry drops in here, he'll then have an 'elluva job to know where he's landed."

"Yes, Dad."

Charlie couldn't help smiling to himself. The Bull and Butcher was a farmhouse by day and a pub by night. They didn't even have a tap room. Only their front parlour, a barrel of ale and an enamel jug. The sign was so old and faded, and the farm so tucked away along the canal, anybody would have a hell of a job to know where they'd landed.

Charlie was in his early 20s. He'd not been called up because he was doing essential farm work. Dad had known Charlie all his life. He was brave and reliable. His mother had died when he was only nine, and he'd had to be his Dad's right-hand man ever since. They were good friends to the boat people, selling them fresh farm produce at fair prices, doing their reading and writing for them, and giving help and advice when asked.

"How will we know he's landed, Charlie?" one old boatman wavered.

"The church bells will ring and the beacons will blaze from the hilltops."

"Do we have to paint out the names on our boats?"

"No, no need. It's names of places, signposts."

"What about the mile stumps along the towpath?"

"Well, the canal company will see to those."

"We don't need no signs and stumps," Dad boasted, "us boatmen have our own landmarks."

Charlie's eyes lit up. "That's how you can all help. You chaps often notice things from the Cut that we can't see from the bank. Keep your eyes and ears open. Report anything suspicious. You know the pubkeepers, lock keepers and village bobbies you can trust."

"We better keep our bike tyres pumped up then", Dad suggested, "in case we have to pedal important messages," Dad said, "and we better notice where all the stop planks are stacked. Case a bomb lands in the Cut."

"Good sense, Alf. How soon do you think they'll come, Charlie?"

"If Hitler misses the bus tonight, he'll have to wait another month till the next full moon."

"Tonight?"

Dad stared at him in dismay. He hadn't realised Jerry was that close.

Toby had been looking from one to the other, following these exchanges with great interest. He didn't understand what they were saying, but he felt the fear, the awful gloom. He heaved a sigh and sunk his chin on Dad's knee in sympathy.

"Oh well, cheer up", old Farmer Green rallied them. "They haven't landed yet. 'Arf an 'our to closin' time! Make the most of it."

But nobody had the heart to delay. They were anxious to get back to their boats, cling to their peaceful way of life while they still had the chance.

"Cowshed." Charlie whispered urgently in Dad's ear as he and Toby were leaving. Toby trotted behind them, following in the wake of Charlie's blacked out lantern. He knew every brick of the old, well-worn path leading up from the farmhouse to the cowshed and farm buildings. Better make sure nobody's skulking about. Charlie swung his lantern into a dark outhouse till he saw yellow eyes, yellow teeth and pounced. Toby had never tackled such a huge rat in his life before. In ten seconds, he'd shaken the life out of it, thwacked its limp body left, right, left, right on the dark

cobbles and laid it, dead, at Charlie's feet.

"Moy hoy, Toby", he laughed, "I'm glad you're on our side."

"He'll search the buildings for you", Dad offered. "Seek, Toby, seek."

Delighted to oblige, Toby scampered into every dusty dark corner of the out-buildings. The barn, store sheds, harness room and the stables where Bob and the Greens' two huge carthorses were fast asleep. He trotted back panting, and settled down patiently to rest at Dad's feet.

Charlie was confiding in an urgent whisper. "The first thing the German paratroopers have been ordered to do when they land here, Alf, is to round up the village Bobby, the vicar, the Sunday school teachers, the village school teachers, the Scout and the Guide leaders, and put them to death. Dad was horrified.

"Why?"

"Hitler's orders. All children are to join the Hitler youth and taught to be Nazis."

"Who does he think he is?"

"Shhh! Keep your voice down." Charlie's voice sank to an even more urgent whisper.

"An awful lot of good, decent living people will have to be

smuggled out of this country. We've already set up escape routes, safe houses, hiding places. Now we want to set up a secret grapevine. It'll be very risky and dangerous. Are you with us?"

"Hide them on my boat, you mean?"

"No, too obvious. All I want you to do is carry secret messages."

Dad's heart sank.

"I can't read and write, Charlie. Never had no schooling."

"Silent messages."

"Silent?"

"A rope coiled in a certain way A certain coloured ribbon tied on the handle of the water can, a windlass or a map out of place. A bunch of corn stalks tucked into Bob's head strap."

"But what will they mean?"

"No need for you to know. Safer that way. You will have to train your family to ask no questions."

The moon suddenly shone forth from behind the huge walnut tree.

"There's no time to lose." Charlie's eyes seemed to burn into Dad's soul. "Are you with us?"

Dad was thrilled to be trusted. He gripped Charlie's outstretched hand hard.

"Course I'm with you."

When Dad got back to the boats, all was still and silent in the moonlight. Mum and the girls were fast asleep. Dad couldn't sleep. He was all churned up inside with all that Charlie had told him. He lay beside Mum fully dressed, his old .410 ready on the cabin floor beside him.

Toby, hoping for a poaching trip, curled up on guard beside the gun. The slide was back. The stars were bright. The sky seemed empty and waiting. A huge tawny owl in the walnut tree started hooting, setting his nerves on edge.

"What if Hitler came tonight? What if the German planes travelled so high, nobody spotted 'em. There'd be no beacons, no bells. They'd all be caught napping."

Dad was determined he wouldn't be caught napping. Towards daybreak, he dozed. He heard the siren in his sleep.

He shot up. The night had changed to a paler dawn. He thought he could hear planes, very faint and far off. Signalling Toby not to make a sound, he picked up his gun and peeped out of the slide. Not a soul, not a sound, not even a cock crow broke the stillness. The whole countryside was fast asleep.

Had he dreamt the siren and the planes? No! He caught the faint throb of German planes. He scanned the skies. Toby, on the cabin top beside him, scanned them too. Suddenly his hackles rose. He gave a low growl. Very high in the pale morning sky, tiny white shapes were drifting down.

Dad steadied his shaking gun on the cabin top, taking aim. "Moy hoy Toby, there's hundreds of 'em."

10

A Letter From Adolf

Papers, papers, everywhere. Along the towpath, in the walnut tree, littering the moored boats and floating on the Cut. Fancy Dad thinking they were parachuters. The girls giggled, arms full of enemy papers. They queued with the rest of the boaters to bundle them into PC Davis's big, hessian mail bag. Toby was having a wonderful time racing hither and thither in the early morning salvage drive, yapping where another batch had drifted down.

PC Davis was the village bobby from nearby Napton on the Hill. He'd known the boat families for years.

"Captain Hone is a very brave man", he told them all as they gathered round him to hear him read what the posters said. "He was ready to stand alone and face the enemy." Dad, scarlet with embarrassment, was glad to be struggling with Toby, who was yap-yapping in his arms, wanting to get back to the White City.

"This 'ere", PC Davis eyed with disdain the soggy bit of paper dripping on the end of his truncheon, is a letter from Adolf Hitler."

"Yap, yap."

"Hitler says we've no chance of winning the war, so we might as well give in."

"Yap, yap."

"He says he's coming to invade us. And when his nice, kind SS troops land, we must do exactly as we are told, and we won't get hurt."

"Yap, yap."

Toby, ignoring their laughter, stuck his little nose in the air, brave and defiant.

"Exactly, Toby."

"Yap, yap."

With utter contempt, PC Davis bundled the paper into the sack with the rest of Hitler's rubbish. Paper was scarce, newspapers were rationed to only a few pages, and everyone had to take their own wrapping paper to the shops. Hitler's rubbish would be pulped into precious new paper.

"Hooray", "Ergh". The cheers and jeers of the small community as they hurried back to their boats to cast off for the day's work, rang out across the countryside. They reached the village up on the hill where the baker was taking loaves of coarse wartime flour from his oven. They reached the blacksmith, shoeing the milkman's pony, and the village school mistress struggling before school opened to mark all the extra work the evacuees brought her. They echoed back across the valley to old Farmer Green, milking the cows in the cowshed behind the Bull and Butcher. They reached Charlie, leading out the two big cart horses with the mower to cut his second crop of hay.

Charlie was singing at the top of his voice "There'll always be an England."

In spite of Hitler's rubbish, England was carrying on as usual.

11

Parcels

All through those July nights, Toby slept beside Dad's gun waiting for invasion, but Hitler missed the bus again. He decided he would first bomb the airfields and cities, and completely destroy the RAF, then he could batter the British people into accepting defeat and invasion. 'Invasion.' Toby couldn't understand this word that everybody was talking about, but he could sense the fear and strain of it, even along the quieter stretches of the Cut, like Napton to Banbury.

The Battle of Britain was being waged night and day. Each morning, the man on the wireless would announce the number of German planes shot down the previous day, and how many British planes were lost or missing. It was a very close score. Our brave airmen were holding the enemy at bay, just. Everybody would pass on the score along the Cut.

Dad never went to sleep at night without checking where the nearest stop planks were, or without his trusty .410 and BB cartridges to hand. He and Charlie snatched every chance they could to practise their secret grapevine.

Mum and the girls soon learned not to question Dad's 'capers', as they called them. But Toby was quite put out if he found anything out of place. Thinking he was being helpful, he'd sit beside it, giving short yaps, drawing everybody's attention to it. Dad would make as if to wallop him; "shut up, you daft a'porth."

Toby, very hurt, would slink away to lick his feelings on the cabin top. No matter how many wallops Dad threatened, he knew when something was amiss or out of place. He knew a lot more than they realised. He knew the secret operational base up in bushy ground where the special auxiliary unit at dead of night had dug and equipped a complete underground bunker for Charlie and his brave resistance workers. He knew which haystacks and ricks were real, and which were camouflaged gun sights and pill-boxes. He knew the dummy bushes hiding neatly stacked gun shells he cocked his leg against along the verges. He spotted the huge tree trunks on wheels, piles of planks, barrels and bollards left handy for road blocks, the smoke pots for smokescreens and even the dummy aluminium works built out in the fields some distance from the real aluminium factory in Banbury.

Hitler was now sending far deadlier mail than his flimsy propaganda letters, especially when the boats were down the north near Coventry, Birmingham and the industrial Midlands.

Parachute flares in long metal cases covered in foreign writing, which turned night into day and guided the German bombers to their targets. Sticks of bombs, three or five in a row, counted with mounting fear as they landed nearer and nearer. Most of all, Toby hated the hundreds of parcels of incendiary bombs flinging their flaming, stinking oil all among the boats and the warehouses.

Dad was worried that an incendiary might land on their cargo of coal or in the empty wooden holds and ignite the boats. Coal, not being a perishable cargo, was not usually sheeted up. For some time, mainly to prevent pilfering, they'd been sheeting up the boats when loaded.

"From now on", Dad decided after a particularly close escape, "we'd better cover up the holds when empty too. We won't do the full sheeting up, just drape the flats over the top planks when we moor at night. With a bit of luck, if we cop a parcel from 'Itler, it'll roll down the flats and into the Cut."

But the next parcel wasn't from Hitler.

"Parcel for you, Rose", Mr Veater called out of his office, as she walked past on the quay. Rose stopped dead in her tracks. A parcel? In all her twelve years, she had never had even a penny postcard through the post, let alone a parcel. "Mum!" she yelled.

Panic stricken, Mum, Dad, Betty, Toby and all the other boat families came running to her aid.

"Whatever is the matter, Rose?" Mum asked anxiously. Rose stared wide eyed with shock.

"I got a parcel."

"Hold on a minute", Mr Veater called, as they all tried to crowd into his office, "I'm bringing it out."

He set it down on the quay. They all fell back, eyeing it as if it might go off at any moment. But Toby nosed round it excitedly, prancing about, wagging his tail. He knew what it was and who had sent it.

"For Captain Rose Hone of the Rose and Betty", Mr Veater read out to her, "With many thanks from the Cain & Abel". Mr Veater helped her to open it. Oooh! Everyone gasped, very envious. Rose was so overwhelmed. Her eyes shone. She couldn't say a word. Abe had made her a beautiful set of crisp white ropework for the Rose and Bet.

"He's fighting far away now, somewhere in the desert", Mr Veater told them all. "Mr and Mrs Darby have called it a day, hung up their windlass and moored their boats at the end of their garden at Wardle near Nantwich. It'll be up to Abe to decide what he wants to do with them when he comes back from the war."

Rose prayed he would come back. She'd like to thank him one day. She took up each piece of work and studied it. There was a broad plait for the top of the rudder, the 'ram's head', as they called it. And another for the tiller. Another below the tiller, and a big broad one for the tingles. There was a strong round fender for the stern, and a 'swan's neck' to hang down the back of the rudder.

The swan's neck was purely for decoration, but all the others were to protect the woodwork of the tiller and rudder. They took the brunt of any bumps, or soaked up excess water to stop it collecting in the joints and rotting the wood. The rope was good, strong cotton, dazzling white.

"Moy hoy, Rose", Charlie Green teased her when they moored at Napton on their homeward trip. "You'll have to cover that lot tonight, else you'll be summonsed for breaking the blackout!"

Even in the heart of the countryside at Napton, they were near enough to the big city of Coventry for their sleep to be broken by air raid warnings. British bombers had made their first raid on Berlin. Hitler's revenge was ruthless. He sent waves of German bombers to head for British cities. British fighters, darting in and out of the bombers, tried to shoot them down. The sky was ablaze with yellow flares, green verey lights and red tracer bullets; " 'Itler's fireworks", the boat people called them.

That particular trip in August had been the worst so far: raids every night. Tired and dispirited, the Hone family longed for the end of the week to tie up in peaceful old Banbury, catch up on their sleep and enjoy a good Sunday dinner with Gran and Grampy Hone in their cosy home down Factory Street.

Toby looked forward to it too. Granny Dot, Grampy's second wife, Dorothy, always spoiled him with his own share of Sunday dinner. She allowed him to perch on the seat of honour - an old canal boat stool with Nelson's worn black Labrador head painted on it. He was always on his best behaviour under the watchful eyes of the two old photographs up on the wall. Granny Rosetta, Grampy's late wife, in her big black boat bonnet and big hoop earrings, and Nelson sitting nobly erect with a doll bundled on the grass before him to represent the real baby he had rescued from the Cut.

"One day you'll be famous too", Betty often boasted in Toby's ear, but Dad always scoffed.

"Can't see a dilon like him saving nobody from the Cut."

The last day of that homeward trip had started badly. Bob had prised off one of his shoes overnight.

"I'll have to walk him up to the blacksmiths at Napton", Dad said, annoyed at this hold up.

"Ah, there's no blacksmith there now, Alf." Charlie told

him. "He's been called up. You'll have to walk Bob over the fields to Southam. There should be one there somewhere. You'll have to find him."

Dad's heart sank. "Come on, Toby. You can find him."

Toby had a good nose for a blacksmith. He was very partial to hoof parings. They were good for his teeth and bones. He soon scented out the new blacksmith. A rough, shaggy haired gypsy called Tinker. He was sitting in the back of an old Bedford van. Toby instinctively knew Tinker liked dogs. He hopped up into Tinker's van and began nosing in his big poacher pocket. Tinker ruffled Toby's silky ears and fed him scraps of parings from his pocket.

"Where's your forge?" Dad looked about him in amazement.

"I be what you might call a travellin' blacksmith."

"Where's your fire? How'd' you fettle the metal?"

"No need. The shoes come ready made. Cobs, cart horses, donkeys, mules. Every size you can think of." He waved at the neat rows of different sized shoes that Toby was nosing at in the back of the van. In no time at all, Tinker had pared Bob's hoof, tossed the bits for Toby to catch, fitted the shoe and filed it to a neat, comfortable finish.

"Two and a tanner, if you please, sir."

Half a crown; more than Dad had paid in his life. But it was a quicker process, and he was chuffed to be called 'sir'.

"I be the only blacksmith left hereabouts now", he warned Dad in parting, "and I be here only one day a fortnit."

"Travelling blacksmiths and ready made shoes." Mum shook her head at Toby in despair as the White City rippled on its homeward way. "Whatever will they fathom up next, Toby?"

That evening, dusk was already gathering as they entered Cropredy Lock. Mum gave Mrs Adkins, the lock keeper's wife, a weary smile.

"Only four more locks to go."

"Has it been a very bad trip?"

Mum nodded "Raids every night since we last saw you. I'm sick to death of 'Itler and his fireworks."

"We're very lucky round here", Mrs Adkins told her, "we

sometimes hear the distant sirens if the wind is from the north, and we sometimes see a faint glow of fire along the horizon. But so far we've been left to sleep and carry on as usual."

Toby, seeing a bucket of swill set ready for Mr Adkins' pig, hopped off the White City to investigate. He had his fill and went to hop back, forgetting the boat was now lower in the lock than when he'd left it. Nobody knew quite what happened next.

"Toby!", Mum screamed, and snatched him in midair, just saving him from falling between the boat and the lock and being crushed to death. "You daft 'aporth."

Dad shook his fist at him, hopping up and down the lock side beside himself with rage. Toby, terrified, no idea what he had done wrong, leapt from Mum's arms, shot along the top planks and hid himself in the lumber 'ole. Dad glared at Mum.

"He's sunk my best windlass!."

"Well, you shouldn't have laid it on the ground there, Alf", Mum said reproachfully. "You're always nagging the girls 'never lay down your windlass'."

She was right. Dad always tucked his safely away over his shoulder, under his jacket, or stowed it safely away in the monkey 'ole. He had trained the girls always to tuck theirs into their waist. Otherwise, they could easily get mislaid or left behind. He couldn't think what had made him do such a stupid thing as to lay it down by the lock side. He was so lacking in sleep, and worn out plodding on through the raids, he hardly knew what he was doing.

The light was fading fast. Too late now to start dredging the lock.

"That's it," he snapped, still furious. "Tie up here for the night."

"Oh, Dad", Betty burst into tears. "I wanted to get to Banbury to ..."

"I'm not leaving here without my best windlass. Rose, take Bob to the Red Lion's tables. Betty, stop that grizzling."

"But Dad, you promised we'd tie up in Banbury tonight."

"Don't blame me. Blame that dog o' yourn. He shoved it into the lock. I reckon he done it o' purpose."

"Oh, o' purpose", Mum muttered scathingly under her breath.

But she couldn't make out how Toby, usually so nimble on his neat little round paws, could have been so clumsy. Toby, sensing he'd let everybody down, took refuge in the lumber 'ole all night.

Early next morning, Dad and Mr Adkins, with the help of a powerful magnet and a big wooden rake, dredged up the precious windlass.

"'Oorray!" Mum, and the girls watching, gave a feeble cheer.

"Mornin'." They all looked up to see the postman up on the bridge.

"Good job you lot weren't moored at Banbury last night. 'Itler dropped a parcel in the lock and another in the basin. Five hundred pounders."

They looked at each other astounded. Neither they nor the Adkins had heard a thing.

"Any one killed?" Dad asked anxiously.

"No, 'cept a one eyed cat. Windows blown out at the Strugglers Inn and Mrs Malloy's cockerel has lost all his feathers with shock."

"Much damage?" they all wanted to know.

"Basin's not too badly damaged, but the lock's blown to bits."

They all stared at each other and at the muddy dripping windlass Rose was holding at arm's length. If Toby hadn't knocked it into the lock, they would have been moored at Banbury Lock.

"Toby", Dad roared. Toby, wondering what he'd done now, gingerly poked his head above the lumber 'ole. "Toby",

Dad held his arms wide in forgiveness.

Ears flapping, stump wagging, Toby scampered as fast as his little legs would carry him and hurled himself into Dad's arms, licking him all over. As they all patted him, he licked them all over too. Betty ruffled his silky ears.

"Told yer he'd rescue somebody one day, didn't I, Dad? But I never thinked he'd save the lot of us."

12

'Britain Can Take It'

Toby sat on the cabin top at Banbury, supervising the unloading of the White City. Since the bombing of the lock six weeks ago, those boats which usually unloaded at wharves beyond the lock could no longer pass through. All along the bank, all sorts of horse drawn carts and waggons were drawn up to relay the cargoes off the boats, through the cobbled alleys of the town, to the wharves on the other side.

All along the bank, boat crews and wharf men were working hard together, unloading the boats. They were determined to show Hitler that, however many parcels he dropped, "Britain can take it" as the posters said on the bomb sites all over the country. It was heavy, dirty work, unloading tons of loose coal. Two big wooden wheelbarrows were placed on planks across the hold. Mum and Dad, with big Co-op shovels, worked to fill one. Betty and Rose, filling buckets with smaller shovels, helped to fill the other.

When at last the White City and the Rose and Betty were empty, they had to turn the boats around, 'wind' them as they called it, in a very tight space. Then they were poled and pulled by hand along to a mooring place. Then the grand spring clean would begin.

Toby, full of his own importance, nose smudged with coal dust, always trotted along with Dad to the office to collect their pay packet and their next order. Everybody in the office knew Toby of the White City. He could rely on several tasty titbits.

By the time they got back to the boats, Mum was washing down the paintwork, Rose was scrubbing her precious plaits, and Betty was cleaning out Budgie's cage and Sampson's box. Dad stowed the order ticket safely away in the ticket drawer. He gave Mum the boat-keeping money for the next trip's rations. He stowed some money away in the best box under the bed for boat repairs, and then went off to the pub to pay for Bob's stabling.

While he was in the Leathern Bottle having a pint and a chinwag with the landlord, Toby passed the time outside in the alley, whopping the rats. The stupid rats kept to their well-worn flight path between the knacker's yard and the stables. When Dad came out, there he was sitting, proud as punch, a big game hunter with his bag before him.

"Four...five...six rats, Toby, clever lad."

Back to the drawbridge next, to inspect how the rebuilding of the new lock was progressing. Toby, nosing over the edge, supervised a workman cutting '1940' into the new lock face.

"Let's hope it lasts another hundred and fifty years like the last one", Dad laughed.

Toby was delighted to find his friend Mr Plester the blacksmith still in business, working in his ancient smithy at the boatyard.

"How's business", Dad asked.

"Non-stop, Alf." He threw Toby a rind of hoof paring. "Everybody's going back to horse power because of the petrol rationing." He lowered his voice. "If you're still looking out for another boat horse, you'd better get one quick."

Dad laughed. "Why, are they rationing horses now?"

Mr Plester nodded, perfectly serious, "Yes, you've got to have a licence from now on to buy a horse. The old ones are needed for horse meat and the young ones wanted for war work."

Toby was nosing round a pile of shiny metal reels.

"That's our war work", Mr Plester said. He looked round to make sure nobody else was in earshot and confided. "When the kids are at school, the Missus and me punch miles of rivet holes into miles of metal tape. I reckon they use it to bind up boxes of munitions. Don't ask me where." He pointed to the poster on the wall behind him, 'Careless talk costs lives'. "They just dump the reels out, and take the finished reels away."

All along the towpath, crews were still busy in the late autumn sunshine, cleaning boats, dollying washing, splicing ropes and polishing brasses. Toby nodded "How do" to every boat dog along the way. Most of them, like the Kent boy's Terry or the Grantham's Curly, were too old to be tempted off the deck for a scrap or a romp. One new little scruffy terrier, bombed out from Nuneaton way, was game for a chase. Toby led him a merry course, doubling to and fro along the towpath, flying over mooring ropes and round and round the standpipe till at last he flopped out, panting in the puddle under the tap. Just as he was lying there, having a lovely roly-poly in the water, all four legs in the air, bursting with the joy of life, the siren went. Everybody groaned and hurried back to their boats. They were all getting fed up with these daylight hit and run or 'scolded cat' raids, as they called them.

In the cities, there were full scale raids with bombers running the gauntlet of British fighters at anti-aircraft batteries. Out in the countryside, it was usually a rogue bomber, a daredevil young German pilot, taking advantage of the British fighter planes engaged elsewhere. He'd fly inland as far as he dare, drop a reckless bomb or two, and race back to base.

Dad could already hear the sinister throb, throb, throb of the lone German plane in the direction of the Market Place. He hurried back with Toby to be with Mum and the girls on the White City.

"They've gone to the market to get the rations", somebody shouted. The Market Place! Dad's heart missed a beat. "Come on, Toby."

Mum could clearly see the bomber coming straight for the market, so low she could see the young pilot. She pushed the girls under a hardware stall, a hail of bullets whipped past her, scattering piles of enamel plates, shattering china chamber pots. As the plane screamed over his head, Dad grabbed Toby and flung himself to the foot of the alley wall.

They watched the plane climb over the town hall clock and bank steeply back down towards the market again. Garrump! The ground shuddered and shook the chime of the town hall clock. A terrible reek of gas filled the air. Frantic with worry, Dad clung to Toby, praying that Mum and the girls were safe. In less than five minutes, it was all over. The bomber fled. The "all clear" wailing forth.

Toby, nose to the ground, led Dad to the Market Place and straight to Mum and the girls still huddled under the stall.

"Toby, Dad!"

The girls scrambled out into Dad's safe, strong arms. Mum stayed still. Toby, whining, nuzzled her. Dad kicked away the shards of broken china, and peered anxiously at her.

"Lizzie, you hurt?"

Mum slowly crawled out and sat, hat askew, on the cobbled Market Square. Trembling, she felt herself all over. Then she saw her brown paper carrier bags of shopping peppered all over with neat, burnt bullet holes.

"Cheeky young devil." She looked up at the ring of anxious faces, all peering down on her. "He were a smokin' a cigarette."

"Pity 'e didn't blow himself up", Dad said later that evening, when they heard that the gas works had been hit, killing two of the workers, badly damaging a gasometer and the nearby railway marshalling yard. He sank down heavily on the side bed in the cabin of the White City.

"I don't feel I ought to dress up and go for a knees-up at the Struggler's Inn tonight, Lizzie. It don't seem right somehow with them poor chaps lying killed."

"You've got to go", Mum said, getting his embroidered boaty belt and braces out of the best box under the bed.

"Them poor chaps would've wanted you to carry on as usual. 'Britain can take it.' It's important." She helped him to buckle on the traditional gear she'd so lovingly stitched for him when they were first married. She caught Toby's bright eyes watching them with interest from the top of the cabin steps. "'Britain can take it', eh Toby?"

Toby, seeing Dad geared for a special evening at the pub, wagged wholeheartedly.

That evening, he sat squashed between Dad and Grampy Hone on the window seat in the Strugglers Inn. Nobody minded that the window had been blown in yet again. The boatmen had rallied around Mrs Soden, the innkeeper's wife, to clean up the debris and build up a wall of sandbags on the pavement outside, so that this plugged the gap behind the dusty blackout curtains. Mr Soden, her husband, was in the fire service. His unit was sent all over the country to fight the fires in the raids in the different cities. Like many an other wife, Mrs Soden had to manage on her own.

Though brick and plaster dust had settled on copper and brass ornaments, they still glowed in the cheerful firelight in the inglenook. The room was full of life, music and colour. Grampy Hone, in the festive faded belt and braces Granny Rosetta had made him many years ago, played jigs on his squeeze-box. Dad beat out a lively rhythm with his shiny spoons, and the boatmen sang and danced their worries away.

When Dad eventually got up to dance, Toby stretched himself into the extra space, and settled for a quiet snooze. From time to time, he opened an eye to check that Dad's dancing boots were still striking sparks from the old stone flags. The ghosts of generations of dancing boatmen filled the old inn around him. The familiar sense of home, boats, ropes, coal, Cut, baccy, beer, tar and towpath wafted over him. He heaved a sigh of bliss. He was a very contented little boat dog.

13

News of the World

" 'Itler thre... threatens to wipe out every town in Britain. Heavy raids on Sar... Southampton and Ply-mouth."

Granny Dot was struggling to pick out words from the meagre few pages of the News of the World. The pale October sunlight slanted through the strips of safety tape stuck to the windows. It was three weeks since the bomb on the gas works. After a good Sunday dinner, Toby was sitting with the rest of the family around the cosy range in Grampy's parlour down Factory Street. They watched Granny Dot listening for every word. "Man buries murdered wife in rubble. Oh, I say!"

Granny Dot was scholar'd. She'd been educated right up to ten years old. She was not a boatwoman. She was born on the bank. Before she married Grampy Hone, she was rather ugly, and painfully shy. Her two front teeth stuck straight out like tusks.

It was very expensive in those days to have dental surgery. Grampy Hone loved her for the person she was. For a wedding present, he paid for the two ugly teeth to be taken away and two neat false teeth fitted. What a difference; she was almost pretty. It was the kindest gift she had ever been given in her life. Though she was not a boatwoman like Granny Rosetta had been, she bravely crewed for Grampy on the Cylgate. But best of all, she loved their little home on the bank down Factory Street. Wisely, she kept it just as it had been in Granny Rosetta's day. The range, pride of Coalbrookdale, glowed in all its glory of cast iron and polished brass. The mantelpiece with its handsome mantle runner trimmed with lace and beadwork was crowded with all the boating mementos that meant so much to the family gathered round her.

"Bookingham Palace hit."

"Ah, was the King and Queen at home?" Mum asked anxiously.

Granny peered at the page. "No, they was a visiting the bombed areas."

"Yah boo to Hitler" Rose laughed at Betty. "Betty went a visiting the bombed areas", Betty gloated, and they all agreed.

"Poor old Coventry's had it again", Granny read. "Rex Picture Palace wiped out."

"Empty, thank the Lord, Mr Sodon told me," Grampy spoke up from his big armchair "that only the front wall of the Picture Palace were left standing. All the posters and film star photos still there, and nothing behind it."

"What was on?"

"Gone with the Wind."

They all laughed. But in their hearts they were not laughing. They knew only too well from the terrifying rage they'd already come through down the north and the rage to face again down the north is next trip, it was no laughing matter. But as Mum kept saying, "If you didn't laugh, you'd have to cry."

"Ford's hospital hit", Granny continued reading. "Firewomen, firewomen!, policemen, wardens lost their lives. 6335 people killed so far. 8690 injured. People pouring out of the city at night camping out in the countryside to get a night's sleep."

"That reminds me", Grampy butted in, "Mr Sodon says watch your flats round Coventry. Somebody's pinching them orf the boats and selling them for ground sheets."

Toby gave a low growl and they all laughed. Betty hugged him. "You'll see 'em orf if they come pinching our flats, won't you Toby?"

But Toby had heard somebody approaching the front door. Nosey as ever, he nipped down off his stool and went with Dad to see who it was. It was one of Mr Plester's many children.

"Please, Captain Hone. Dad says can you come to the stables quick."

Rose panicked. "Is it our Bob? Can I come with you, Dad?"

"Stop here, all of ya. I'll come straight back"

If anything had happened to old Bob, Dad had to face it alone. Stealing himself for the worst, he hurried away. Toby, hairs on end sharing his master's dread, scurried along over the cobbles beside him.

Within half an hour, Dad and Toby were back. The others were still round the fire, just as he'd left them. Toby, full of his own importance, hopped back on his stool and looked to Dad to break the news.

Dad dumped a set of small harness on the table, took a deep breath, and bravely announced: "I've buyed a mule."

"What's happened to our Bob?" Rose cried in horror. "You won't let nobody eat him, will you Dad?"

"Nah, Bob's fine."

"What you buy the mule for, then?" Mum demanded.

"He were cheap."

"If he's cheap, Alf" Grampy put in, "he's no good."

"What about your licence?" Granny reminded.

"Don't need no licence for a mule. He'll be fine once we built him up."

"Built him up?" Mum echoed shrilly.

"He's got right down", Dad explained. "He were frit by the whistle of a train going along tunnel straight. Pinned his chap to the wall. Chap thrashed him all the way to Banbury, then dumped 'im in Tooleys' stables. Nobody knowed he was in there.

Three 'ole days in the dark without even a drink of water. Blacksmith Plester and Farmer Knott found him, told the chap 'e ought to be reported to the cruelty man. Chap told 'em they could chuck the hanimal in the Cut for all he cared. He were orf to a hengine boat."

Dad shook his head sadly at them all.

"You knows how it is. Everybody changing to hengine boats. Nobody don't want boat horses no more."

"What's 'is feet like?" Mum asked dubiously.

"Mr Plester says his feets is good and he's young. If he is

treated proper, there's years of work left in him yet."

"There's years of work left in old Bob." Rose agreed. "We'll never get a better boat horse than our Bob, Dad." Betty's lips trembled. She snuffled her cuggy. "You ain't getting rid of our Bob, are you Dad?

"Oh, it's like this 'ere", Dad perched on the edge of the table. "Our Bob ain't getting any younger."

"He's only eighteen", Mum said. "Grampy's old Champion is thirty-odd."

"If this winter is as bad as the last, with so many canal maintenance men away at the war, and the towpaths getting worser and worser, it ain't fair on our Bob coping with both boats all the time. With a back-up hanimal, they can take turn and turn about, or each take a boat. If one's tooked bad, we can leave him with a friendly farmer, Farmer Green at Napton or Farmer Knott at Wormy-leighton, and pick him up on the way back.

Dad looked to Grampy for his approval, but Grampy was soon going to retire from boating and felt that from now on, the family must decide for themselves. He did, however, point out: "Look how Dolly is with the Friendship. Joe Skinner reckons Dolly's got more sense than 'im and Rose put together. She's very surefeeted and just as strong as an 'orse; she pulled the Friendship and the Elizabeth for years. Mules don't eat so much, ain't so particular, smaller feet - cheaper to shod."

" 'As he got an 'andle?" Mum asked.

"Jack."

She still looked doubtful. "We ain't never 'ad no mule before."

Dad looked at Toby for support. "You took to Jack, didn't ya Toby?

Toby wagged, basking in Dad's approval.

"Oh well", they all laughed. "If Toby took to him", and that settled it.

Thus Jack the mule became one of the crew with Bob and Toby, and worked faithfully with the Hone family for many years.

The clock on Grampy's mantlepiece struck four. Toby

drummed on his stool with his little front paws, signalling it was time to get home to his White City.

"You'll see, Lizzie" Dad reassured her as he picked up the mule harness. "Jack will be fine once he's 'ad 'is little 'oliday."

" 'Oliday! What's an 'oliday?" Mum had never had a holiday in her life.

"Farmer Knott has offered to look after him on his farm till our next trip. We can pick him up at Knott's Bridge on our way back from down the north.

"Huh", Mum snorted. "I'd like an 'oliday from 'Itler and his fireworks."

Dad sighed. They all knew there was little chance of that in the week to come.

14

Faggots and Peas

Toby lay with his nose pressed under the air raid shelter door at Tusses Bridge. The raid seemed to have been going on for ages. It was long past his bedtime. Despite the heavy rattle of gunfire and the whiffs of dust blasting under the door, he wanted to be out there guarding his White City.

It wasn't much of an air aid shelter. It was only an old brick built hut with sandbags piled round the outside, and bare wooden benches ranged round the wall on the inside. It was only a few miles from the centre of Coventry as the plane flies, and far too close for comfort to the ' 'lectric light', as they called it, the big power station which made electricity for the whole of that important city. At least it gathered all the boat women and children together under one roof to comfort each other, and made it simpler after each raid to account for the dead and injured.

The women and children were huddled in homemade shawls and blankets on the benches. Most of the children had dropped off to sleep, leaning against their mothers. Mum cuddled Betty fast asleep on one side, and Rose struggling to keep awake on the other.

Every now and again there would be an uneasy lull as one wave of bombers fled and the guns died. Toby would snuffle eagerly along the crack, hoping to hear the 'all clear', only to hear the guns opening up again as another wave of bombers approached. His ears drooped. He'd give a great sigh of disgust and sink back on his neat little haunches again.

All through September into October, Hitler, furious that Britain was still holding out against his superior forces, had been sending his bombers over, wave after wave, night after night. He threatened to flatten every important town and city, depriving people of sleep so they'd give in and the invasion would be a walkover.

Coventry was a very important city. It had many factories, including those making munitions and electrical goods for ships and planes, chemicals for important research, and silk for parachutes. The 'lectric light was fuelled by coal brought by the canal boats to Sutton Stop. Big double-barrelled automatic anti-aircraft guns were dug into the earth all round the power station, and made almost as much racket as the bombs. Brave men manned the roof with their machine guns. From time to time, spent bullet cases flurried against the door of the shelter or clattered on the roof. The mothers would stir and open their eyes warily, but the children slept on.

Rose, dead tired, was too frightened to sleep. Her dear Dad was out there somewhere, on fire-fighting duty. Toby, fed up with the stink of the stuffy paraffin heater and the stench of the lavvy bucket in the corner, suddenly decided "enuff was enuff". Every hair on his body was urging him to get back on guard on his White City. Frantically, he began whining and scratching under the door."

"Oh, bring 'im 'ere, Rose, for goodness sake", Mum whispered urgently, "before he wakes the whole boat."

But even at home on Mum's lap, he still had the fidgets. "I suspect it's cause Dad's out there."

Rose's eyes filled with tears. "Why has Dad been on duty three nights running, Mum?"

"There's not enough men to go round, dearie. They're all

battling in the city. Three canal arms meets out there, with wharves and boats all along 'em. Dad and the boat men must patrol and put any fires out quick with the stirrup pumps."

There was another barrage of gunfire.

"At least he's not up on top of that 'lectric light roof with them machine gunners."

Rose whimpered, I ain't 'alf ungry, Mum."

"I know, dearie." Mum cuddled her closer. They were all hungry. "When we gets back home, we'll open up the range and have a nice hot drink."

It was a shame. They'd had little to eat all day as they worked their empty boats to Coventry. They'd been looking forward so much to tying up at Tusses Bridge and having their special local treat: Mrs Simpson's faggot and peas with a generous dollop of hot mashed potatoes. Mrs Simpson lived next door to the Elephant & Castle pub again' the bridge. Like the Sephtons, the Phipkins, Paddy Wilde and all the other boat people that lived along there, she and her husband had retired after a hard life working the boats. She knew only too well how boat crews, after a long day's work on the Cut, appreciated a hot home cooked meal at a reasonable price. The food office allowed her extra rations for this special service.

Early evening, she would come along the moored boats taking the orders. Smelling as she constantly did of food, Toby always gave her a tremendous welcome. At a given time, he would trot purposefully along with Rose and Betty and all the other customers with their assorted containers to queue outside Mrs Simpson's cottage. Then, like the famous Bisto Kids, breathing in the delicious aroma, they would hurry back to the White City to share out the feast.

Usually, the raids started around nine o'clock, but this evening it was much earlier. Mrs Simpson had only just taken the orders from each of the boats for the faggot and peas when the siren blared out.

"Huh? Cheerio, faggot and peas", Mum sighed.

Rose jumped as a bomb landed much nearer. The thunder of the guns was deafening. The light swayed and dimmed. She watched it, terrified. It was only a bare low watt fly blown bulb hanging from a rafter, but it went out. They knew it would mean the 'lectric light had been hit. The bombers throbbed, throbbed, throbbed overhead, shaking the shelter. The guns raged nonstop. Rose clung to her Mum, crying quietly, trying hard to be brave.

"Sing to me, Mum."

Mum laid her cheek against Rose's head, rocking her and singing softly. It was a little chorus the Salvation Army had learned her as a kiddie. "

"Jesus bids us shine with a pure clean light, like a little candle burning in the ..."

They ducked and held their breath as the bomb screamed overhead. Thud! The bulb went out. Toby shot to the door and made himself scarce along it. Mum, stunned for the moment, steeled herself for the almighty explosion that must surely follow. Nothing happened. It must be another unexploded bomb or landmine. She said a little prayer to herself for the brave men who would have to deal with it. She wavered on singing in the dark.

"In this world of darkness, we must shine, you in your small corner and I in mine."

The bulb flickered and came on again. With tremendous relief, she carried on humming and rocking for some time. "Mmmm mmm umm umm."

There was an uncanny lull outside. No guns, no planes. Were the guns cooling off their red hot barrels ready for the next wave of bombers? They strained to hear. There'd been no more bombs since that last tremendous thud.

"Mum", Rose suddenly looked up at her, hardly daring to breathe the words, "I think it's over." They sat quite still listening intently to the beautiful silence.

Toby, paw raised, every hair on end, one ear pressed to the bottom of the door, listened too. "All clear". The hooter boomed out loud and steady. Toby went mad, flinging himself against the door, yapping at Mum to open it. He shot straight out to his White City.

Mum stood at the open door of the hut. The moon made the October night as light as day. She could see Dad and the other boatman trudging wearily back along to their boats. Yet again, they'd all survived. The urgent clang of distant ambulance bells made her sad for those who hadn't. Despite the acrid smell of burning, she marvelled at the great amber bowl of the starry sky reflecting for miles around the fires still raging in the city. Despite the debris floating on the Cut, Tusses Bridge was perfectly reflected in the still peaceful water. "The Cut's still here", she announced to the women in the hut. A weary cheer answered her from all the mothers struggling to rouse their reluctant children. She was amazed to hear a distant clock striking only ten. It seemed as if they had been in there all night long. She was dying for a cup of tea.

Toby inspected his White City. Spent tracer bullets littered the fore deck. But it was all there. He scampered back along the gunwales to the hatches and the cabin. Filthy smuts and charred straw everywhere. But it was all there. He hopped up on to the cabin top along the top planks and stopped abruptly. He knew he should have stayed on guard.

"Oh, what's Toby yapping at?" Mum asked wearily, as they all assembled back on the White City.

"He's telling you some sneaky devil's pinched our best flat."

Dad leaned heavily on the cabin top, his head on his arms, totally disgusted.

"Oh, poor Toby." Betty, still half asleep, drew him into her arms for comfort. "I shouldn't have dragged you away to that shelter."

A new flat would cost a lot of money, but it wasn't only the cost. It was the meanness of the act that knocked the stuffing out of them all.

"Never mind", said Mum. "We'll all have a nice 'ot cuppa... Oh, no", she gave way to tears. The range was out. It was the last straw.

"No range, no flat, no faggots."

Rose, realising how much all her family meant to her, put her arm round her mother.

"Never mind, Mum. We're all here."

Toby suddenly sniffed the air. Yelping with delight, he leapt from Betty's arms and scampered along towards the bridge. Out of the amber twilight waddled a beautiful vision - Mrs Simpson in her old felt hat and long white apron carrying two steaming cauldrons of food.

"Who ordered faggot and peas?"

15

Bomb in the Cut

Two days later, Granny Lunn waved goodbye to them as they set off on their homeward trip. They were lucky to have her living at Atherstone. She had retired from the boats and lived on the bank in a house belonging to the coal company. She was the one who looked after Betty's rabbits in her backyard. She always took in Mum's washing if the weather was bad. She would have it all ready washed and ironed when they called on their next trip. She always sent them on their homeward journey with something home-made to eat on the way. This morning she had made them a big rabbit pie and a big bake of bread pudding. She knew there would be no extra treats like faggot and peas until they'd saved enough money to replace the stolen flat.

Toby lifted his nose and licked the rain from his whiskers. He stood on the cabin top beside Mum at the tiller, and gazed proudly out beyond their neatly sheeted cargo. October was running out with a damp raw air, and a steely grey Cut pitted with raindrops. Despite the last two nights of raids on Atherstone and Nuneaton, everybody was remarkably cheerful.

"Nice morning", Mum greeted passing crews.

"Nice morning", they grinned back.

Toby loved this busy stretch of their homeward journey from the mine at Baddesley to the junction at Sutton Stop. All down the Atherstone locks right down to the stone quarries at Mancetter and Hartshill, the grapevine was buzzing with the latest news of the war. So far that month, the total of German bombers shot down far exceeded the number of British fighters lost. Despite the constant raids on our cities, replacement aircraft were coming off the production lines night and day. At last, our brave British airmen were slowly but surely winning the Battle of Britain. There was even a wonderful rumour that Hitler was having to postpone the invasion till the spring.

Toby looked back to see if the girls were all right. Now the Rose and Bet was heavily laden with coal, she was on a long tow rope. The girls would have to take it in turns at the tiller all the way to Sutton Stop, then all the way to Banbury.

Rose sighed as the red dust from the quarries gathered on her wet paint work. It was borne on the drizzle from the red topsoil of the quarries. More and more stone was needed to mend bombed runways and to build new ones. Toby wagged his tail at the queue of boats two abreast, waiting to be loaded at the stone wharves.

Dad flipped the drips from his cap and sighed. There wasn't a horse drawn pair amongst them.

"Nice day." They smiled indulgently at his old-fashioned menagerie. Dad didn't mind. Let 'em smile. He'd have Jack the mule as well next trip. He was still proud to be a horse-drawn number one. He wasn't selling out to the big carrying companies just to get a free hengine boat. He stroked Bob's long, wet nose.

"Bob old sport, you're still the bestest hengine on the Cut."

Was it true that Hitler was postponing his invasion till the spring? Dad hoped so. It would give Charlie and his resistance workers extra time, not only for the secret grapevine, but also to set up the chain of safe bolt-holes where innocent victims could be hidden. And the ports from which they could be smuggled out of the country. Dad was so proud to be one of Charlie's trusted band. He eyed the captains of the other boats that passed, wondering which of them was a trusty too. Boats on their way to the mines, mills and ports of the north, boats travelling south with their cargoes of coal, stone, ingots of metal, boxes of ammunition, sacks of wheat and tins of Spam.

Toby eyed every boat dog that passed. Dogs on cabin tops and counters. Dogs on planks and fore-decks. Dogs slumped precariously on all sorts of cargoes. Hardly any of them had a collar. Toby had a very smart collar, crocheted by Mum so Betty could tie a rope on him when they went for a walk. He viewed everything with a lively interest and perfect balance as the White City rocked up and down on the constant wash from chugging engines.

By late afternoon, the red dust and conveyor belts of the stone quarries had given way to the black dust and slag heaps of the coal fields. Toby sneezed at the pungent coal tar smell of wet coal.

Betty, taking her turn at the tiller, watched the black dust settling on the wet paint work, swirling in eddies along the edge of the Cut and saturating the black mud of the towpath. A steady traffic of laden boats emerged from the side-arms of the different mines: the Griff, the Measham, the Charity, the Newdigate and others. Hard coal for steam trains and machinery, cobs for baker's ovens, beans for the great paper mills, dusty sweepings for the cement works and nutty slack for power stations.

Toby barked at a passing load of nutty slack. Mum laughed at the steerer. "Just 'cause he's carrying best house coal, he thinks he's a cut above the rest."

By the time they'd reached Sutton Stop, the rain had eased; a foggy dusk was closing in. Rose led Bob over the horse bridge while Mum and Dad and Betty worked the boats round the tricky bend from the Coventry Canal on to the Oxford.

"You're the last boats I shall loose through today", Mr Veater told them as he carefully gauged the White City in the stop lock. "The Home Guard will be dropping the stop planks across here after you. They drop them in every night now."

Toby was supervising him as usual.

"Glad to see old bossy boots is still with you", he laughed.

"Oh, couldn't manage without him", Dad laughed back and he was surprised to realise that he meant it.

Bob, tired of waiting to be hitched back on the tow rope, sauntered off to the Greyhound stables for the night. Rose ran and fetched him back.

"I reckon Bob's had enough, Dad. Can we tie up here for the night?"

Dad was tempted. There was nothing he'd enjoy more than a good old chinwag with his fellow boatmen in the Greyhound. But it was perilously close to the 'lectric light.

"Shouldn't think there'd be a raid tonight, Alf", Mum said, "not with this fog coming down. What do you think, Mr Veater?"

Betty, anxiously snuffing her cuggy, looked to him, longing for him to agree.

"Ah, I should push on", he advised. "It's less than a mile to Tusses Bridge. If the Home Guard drop the stop planks across there, they might hold you up in the morning."

After a good supper of Granny Lunn's rabbit pie, they were all glad to snatch an early night. Mum and the girls were already asleep by the time Dad had finished a leisurely shave.

"Thank the Lord for fog and a good night's sleep. Night, Toby." He patted his precious shaving mug safely into place on the shelf. Toby, curled upon the floor beside Dad's gun, looked up at him devotedly.

"Night, Toby." Dad patted him too, and ruffled his ears with rough affection. Toby, knowing he was loved, gave a blissful sigh and curled up to sleep.

Midnight. The sirens went. Almost immediately the guns opened up.

Drugged with sleep, Dad automatically pulled his clothes on over his night shirt, stowed everything from the cabin top into the cabin and helped Mum to drag the sleepy girls from their warm bed into cold boots and coats. The first bomb fell. Snatching up shawls and blankets, they stumbled along to the shelter with the rest of the boatwomen and children. The fog had gone. It was a clear, frosty night.

Crouched against the chimney on his cabin top, Toby kept a watch on the White City. The raid was different from usual. He soon sensed a pattern to the explosions. The bombs were dropping in sticks of three.

One … two … **BANG!**

"Bomb in the Cut!", yelled a distant voice.

Smack! Toby hit the ice-cold water, paddling for his life, fighting for breath, he was sucked and swirled away into the darkness.

16

'O Where, O' Where'

" 'ave you seen a little white dog with a stumpy tail and wide ears?"

"Have you seen our Toby?"

"Have you seen Toby of the White City?"

After vowing there'd be no holding up the boats if ever Toby was missing, it was Dad who couldn't leave without searching for him.

Crowds of sightseers were gathered round Mr Veater and the canal workmen, surveying the huge, muddy hole where the Cut had been. A sickly sweet smell of rotting vegetation hung on the frosty air.

The bomb had fallen on the towpath, breaking the bank between the stop lock and Tusses Bridge. It must have lifted the boats out of the water, cargo and all. It was a wonder they hadn't broken their backs. The crews found the heavy mooring rings wrenched from the bank, and pots and pans strewn all over cabin floors.

Betty had found Budgie clinging to the corner of his overturned cage, his little heart thumping, fit to burst. And Samson was gibbering with fright, pulling his long pink tail through and through his tiny pink claws in great agitation. Dad had discovered his precious Toby mug under the bed. It had fallen on the rag rug and wasn't broken, thank goodness. But the real Toby was nowhere to be found.

"Where would all this water have finished up, Mr Veater?"

"Well, some of it would have got away in the condit, Alf."

"You mean that big iron pipe where the children love to hide and shout in the summer."

"In the summer it's dry. In flood, it carries excess water

away to waste ground, old brick ponds and old mine workings and such like. But the condit was damaged last night."

"Brian", he called to him a young lad about seven years old, looking for eels in the mud with several other children.

"This is Sam Phipkin's grandson. You know old Sam Phipkin, the boatman", Mr Veater told Dad, "he was bombed out by the same stick of bombs. Alderman's Green Road. All survived, thank the Lord."

"Our house caught the second bomb," Brian told Dad. "The third must have hit the Cut. We were in the Anderson shelter. We heard this terrible roaring noise under the earth. We didn't know it was the Cut running away. The Crown took us in." He grinned as if it were a huge adventure. "I slept on their billiard table."

Dad described Toby, asking Brian if he'd seen him. Brian shook his head.

"Promise me", Dad said, "if you see or hear anything of him, you'll tell Mr Veater. His name's Toby. Toby of the White City."

"Toby of the White City." Brian promised.

"He's a reliable little lad", Mr Veater assured Dad as Brian ran back to play with the other children. "I'm keeping an eye on all of them while the mothers find out where they're going to sleep tonight. A dozen of them use that Anderson shelter. I expect relations will put them up for a few days, but goodness knows where they'll all find accommodation after that."

"I'll have to scort orf." Dad had yet to collect Bob from the stables of the Elephant and Castle. "How long do you think this lot'll be out of order, Mr Veater?"

"Well, the pile driving team are on their way, so about a week by the time the tow path's restored."

Dad shot him a last pleading glance.

"You will get the message about our Toby out on the grapevine, won't you?"

"I'll do my best, Alf."

Mr Veater didn't hold out much hope if Toby had been swept away with the Cut. An underground stream ran under the canal into the River Sow. The River Sow ran into the Severn and the Severn ran to the open sea.

17

Tike

The next night, while yet another raid was pounding Coventry, a creature, more dead than alive, oozed out in smelly black slime from a big, empty iron pipe. Slowly, it slithered down the steep, muddy embankment and landed shivering in one of the city's rubbish dumps. The noise of the raid a few miles away was now muffled beyond the high edge of the pit. A haze of thick smoke hung in the air. Rubbish some way off was well alight from the scattering blazing oil of an incendiary bomb. Stinking warmth spread through ash and clinker. It rekindled the spark of life still left in the creature.

It had been swept away by flood, side-swept into a broken conduit, struggled through debris and darkness to the draught of air beyond, and ended up in a rubbish dump. But it was not beaten yet. It struggled to lift its head. It had wide, filthy ears. It couldn't see or smell very well. Its eyes and nose were bunged up. Tshoo! Tshoo! Again and again, it sneezed. It stopped. It scented home. Home! Whimpering with delight, he struggled and dragged himself over the rubbish. He came to a patch of clear ground. He rubbed his eyes along it. Then he saw it. A ramshackle lean-to of old sacks and tarpaulins, tied to a thicket. He crawled in. The ground sheet was his stolen flat! Memories of his dear family and happy boat home filled him with joy. He rolled and rolled, and then was violently sick all over it.

"Filthy Tike!", a lordly voice rent the air. A huge hand held back the canvas flap. A terrifying god of a man with wild hair and massive beard loomed against the fiery sky, with one lift of his sandalled foot.

"Out".

Toby sailed through the air and landed back in the rubbish dump. He lay there for a while, gazing at the stars and getting his breath back. He was very empty and very thirsty. He foraged around. Recent rain had left puddles in old tin cans, chipped enamel bowls and rusty containers. There was plenty of food, all stamped 'unfit for human consumption'. Toby tried this and that, some gritty with bomb damage, some contaminated by broken sewers or sodden by firemen's hoses. What didn't suit, came straight back.

Eventually, satisfied after trial and error, he crept back over the rubbish to keep an eye on his flat. It had been cleaned up and cast outside for the night. Beside it stood a deep old-fashioned wooden perambulator piled high with rubbish.

The man was moving about in the semi-light with slow deliberate steps. He was very old. His hair and beard seen dimly against the dark of the tent, were a dirty white. His beard was tremendous, starting under his eyes and trailing almost to his knees. He wore an officer's old greatcoat of the First World War. Around his neck was what had once been a gent's white silk evening scarf. Ragged sacks hung below his coat like tattered skirts. His legs were bound with strips of sacking. Though it was nearly November, he wore no socks

and clumsy home-made sandals stitched from old horse harness. He was very strong. Slowly, methodically, he emptied the pram, flinging the contents some distance away.

In the flickering light from the dwindling fires on the dump, piles of junk could be seen. A heap of old bicycle and pram wheels. A stack of big square rusty biscuit tins overflowing with bits of old rope, string and scraps of binder twine. A mound of mouldy broken harness. Piles of wood and coal and a rank of rusty iron ranges and cooking stoves. The smell of paraffin and stew mingled in the smoky air. One of the oil stoves was alight with a steaming pot on the top.

When at last huge snores came from within the shack, Toby crept over and once again spread himself blissfully on his flat.

In the morning, the man towered over him, fiercely contemplating him and all the rats Toby had caught in the night.

"You've got a valuable dog there, Arky", a cheeky voice shouted down from the edge of the dump.

"Yeah", a second voice echoed. "Government's offering a big reward for a dog like him, Arky."

Snatching up an iron bar, in shaky self-defence, the old man glowered up at the figures against the skyline. Two cheerful dustmen were standing in the back of an old Bedford ash lorry shovelling out the last of the rubbish into the tip. Bantering the old la-di-da tramp was obviously a regular game.

"It's National Rat Week, Arky, masses of bombed out rats are running all over the country. Count up the rats he catches and he could be a national champion."

"Yeah, make yourself a fortune, Arky. Posh up your egg waters no end. They are proper hofficer gent. "Where'd you pinch him from, Arky?"

Arky shook his iron bar at them.

"Ooh, temper, temper," they mocked.

Toby yapped at them to go away.

"Nice doggy, 'ere doggy, 'ere doggy", they invited.

"Stay Tike," Arky commanded in a deep, rich voice. Toby stayed.

At last, tired of baiting the surly old tramp, the men cranked the engine of the lorry into life with the starting handle, and bumped away out of sight.

Late that night, Arky trundled his wooden ark of a perambulator into the grounds of a gaunt empty mansion. It was well hidden behind trees. Toby, tied to the handle of the pram on a length of binder string, was tired out. They had trundled miles, well out of sight of people which Arky regarded as 'the enemy', along field paths and waste ground, skirting farms and old coal mines. At one joyful point, they'd even crossed the canal. Toby tugged towards it. Arky yanked him back. Toby was puzzled. The canal was deserted. No sound of boat people, no sign of boats, no scent of cosy chimneys smoking into the crisp night air.

Arky kept Toby tethered. He had spotted 'enemy' posters in all sorts of out of the way places. "National Rat Week starting Monday, November, the 4th" they said. "This is another war we must win", they said, "every man, woman and child to become a rat reporter. Is your dog a champion rat catcher? Reward." Arky hadn't bothered to read about the reward. He wanted no reward, only a rat catcher. He wanted no attention whatsoever from 'the enemy'.

"Better lie low for a week or two. No nightly forays into the ruins of the city. Bivouac here, well away from headquarters."

The deserted mansion had been built a century before for a wealthy mine owner. He'd sited it close to his mine. Coal was everywhere on the surface. It had no gas, electricity or running water. Arky didn't attempt to break in. He hated a solid roof over his head. He'd obviously been there several times before. He brought all he needed in his ark. He set up camp round the back of the house among dilapidated greenhouses and potting sheds. There was a handy well and a small iron furnace that had once heated the greenhouses.

Here he made his bivouac. He hooked the eyelet holes on Toby's flat over the strong line of hooks he'd screwed into the near side of the ark. It draped down and extended as a ground sheet. The makeshift roof was another tarpaulin and this was fixed to the hooks on the far side, draped over the ark, keeping the contents dry, and extended shelter beyond the ground sheet. It was fixed to the ground expertly with guy strings and homemade tent pegs. Under there, Arky was as snug and dry as in a proper tent.

Toby had tried to crawl into the tent too. At first, Arky kept shoving him out. But before a week was up, Toby had staked his claim. "After all", he seemed to say, as he wriggled in bottom first, "this is my flat". He wasn't going to be parted from his flat. It was his only link with home and loving kindness. Arky showed no kind feelings towards him, never patted him or ruffled his ears. Hardly spoke, except to give a curt command. Gave him minimum of food and shelter and little freedom, except to catch rats.

One cold November afternoon, Toby howled with loneliness. He'd been tied to the pram handle at the back of the mansion for hours. Arky had lumbered off into the woods to tend his wires for rabbits. They'd been camping there for three weeks. Toby longed for the freedom and bustle of his life on the White City. He pined for all his dear gang: Mum, Dad, Bob and the girls with their lively chatter, their fussing and petting. It seemed ages since he'd heard a young voice, seen a young person.

As if by magic, a young lad suddenly appeared clutching a large eiderdown and pillow to his chest. He stopped with amazement when he saw the lonely little dog shivering with cold, tied up to a most peculiar pram.

"Not round there, Brian", an unseen voice called him back.

Toby, overjoyed to see Brian, shot to the end of his tether, wagging his tail and yelping with delight. Brian stared hard at the dog. Wide ears, stumpy tail, no doubt about it. This must be the little boat dog lost from the White City.

"Hello, Toby."

Toby went berserk, prancing, begging him to free him, take him home. Brian longed to hold him, but his arms were full.

"Back in a minute", he promised.

"Mum." Clutching his bedding, he raced round to the front of the house. Brian's mother, Mrs Liggins, was busy supervising a stream of women and children carrying household goods and bedding from the back of an ARP lorry in through the front door of the mansion.

"Oh, not now, Brian", she pleaded as he begged her to come and look round the back. "We must get these rooms allocated. There's a lot more bombed out families arriving in a minute. It's a full moon tonight. We must get the cellar turned into a shelter before blackout."

The damp, gloomy mansion echoed with children's stamping boots, and excited voices. Brian strode up the bare stairs two at a time, dumped the bedding on the dusty floor in his family's room, and raced back out again to rescue Toby. But only Toby's broken tether, dirty bits of binder string knotted together, remained.

That night, Toby was back with Arky in the noisy city. The raid was the worst Coventry had had. Toby crouched under the pram as a bomb whistled overhead. He squeezed his eyes shut, waiting for the bang. He buried his nose in his paws as shrapnel rained down.

It wasn't shrapnel. It was shallots. It was raining vegetables. Shallots, carrots, potatoes, hailed down, bouncing among the broken bricks all over the road. The greengrocers at the end of the street had been hit. The pram was already half full of treasures Arky had looted from sagging garden sheds and gaping cellars. But he wasn't leaving this bounty behind. "Fetch, Tike." Toby enjoyed running to and fro delivering them into Arky's huge, open palms.

The greengrocers was well alight now. There was nobody to report it. The back-street was deserted. Every fireman, policeman, warden, was streets away, fighting the raging fires in the city centre. The beautiful ancient cathedral towered like a flaming torch into the night sky, its vast lead roof running away down the cobbled street like molten lava.

The pram was full. Time to withdraw to headquarters. Arky tied Toby to the handle. With slow, purposeful tread, eyes straight ahead, oblivious to the racket of guns and bombs, the stench of broken sewers and gas mains, Arky vanished into the smoke, trundling his ark before him.

18

Fireman Bill

That same night, several hours later, only a few streets away from the burnt out greengrocers, Leading Firewoman Elsie Anker bent to her dangerous task with a steady hand in the middle of the city. The raid was at its height. She had driven through it with 150 gallons of petrol in the back of her fire station van. There was no other person, no other vehicle available to get the cans of petrol through the battered city to the six fire engines cut off in the middle of the city. This was the last appliance now, no time to switch off its engine. The pump must be kept going at all costs. Her tin hat, close to the pounding heat and fumes of the running engine felt like a ton weight. Fear drenched her in sweat. The glowing hot exhaust manifold lay only inches from the petrol filler cap. With utmost control and concentration, she poured steadily into the petrol tank.

"You spill one drop on that hot manifold", a passing fireman warned her as she carried the last can of petrol from the van, "you and that pump will be blown to kingdom come."

As if she didn't know. She knew exactly what he'd say next: "We can manage without you, but there's not another pump for miles around."

She carefully emptied the last drop, replaced the filler cap and almost fainted with relief. Her legs were like jelly as she picked her way over snaking hoses and steaming puddles to report to the Control Officer. She had to shout to make herself heard above the roar of the fires and the din of the throbbing engine.

"Duty completed, sir."

The control officer saw a slight figure in a firewoman's

uniform. Tin hat awry, face smudged with oil, flushed with heat and sweat; his face in the firelight filled with admiration.

"You deserve a medal, lass."

"The telephone lines are still down, sir. Any further messages to take back to the station?"

Whoosh!

They both jumped back as something landed in the fire, shooting a flight of sparks up in the intense heat. He mopped his brow under his helmet.

"God help us if the water runs out."

Elsie sat in the van for a moment before she started back. She had to ignore the raid, and gather her wits about her. Several of the roads she had come on would now be impassable. She tried to work out the best route to take. On her nippy despatch bike, she could thread through almost anywhere. But it was not going to be so easy with this van and its blacked out headlights. She started the engine and eased slowly past the hoses.

"Not again."

Yet another warden's hand halted her.

"You can't get through this way, Miss, unexploded land mine. You'll have to go back. I'll guide you."

Wearily, she tried another road, only to find it blocked by a flaming gas main. A rattle of spent machine gun bullets landed on the bonnet. Fireworks were still shooting full blast overhead.

All those months of training in the phoney war learning every little back road and alleyway of the city on their messenger dispatch bikes now paid off. There was still one more little back street she might get through. In contrast with the blazing light in the city centre, the street was very dark. Every few yards, she hopped out and took her torch to inspect the way ahead. The dimmed beam caught the dark mass of a fallen tree. A glimpse of white amongst it was a little dog on guard.

"You still on duty too?"

Toby, overjoyed to hear her kind voice, shivered all over, longing to wag a welcome. But he was all caught up in the tree. She soon cut him free. He whined and sniffed at the tree, telling her something else was under there. She shone her torch among the branches. Ah, she'd know that beard anywhere. It was that thundering nuisance Arky, the bane of the city's police and emergency services, always poking around where he shouldn't. Ah, he was stone cold. Must have happened hours ago. There was nothing she could do for him. She shone her torch to see how far the tree lay across the road. She could just squeeze past it with the van.

"Come on, sweetheart."

The little dog sat adamant, willing her to notice something else. She shone her torch and spotted it. The fallen tree was only a large branch. The rest of the tree was still standing. Hanging precariously on the lowest branches was a parachute bomb. Any vibration from the van could set it off.

They couldn't go back. They had to go on. She walked carefully past the branch, noting every brick and pothole for some distance ahead.

"If we go, we go together", she said grimly, lifting the little dog on to the passenger seat. It immediately sat up and took a lively interest. It was obviously used to travelling.

She was dead tired, but the same iron nerve that had seen her through the petrol ordeal had to be summoned up again. With tremendous stealth and concentration, she inched past

the branch. Slowly, very slowly, she edged round the dips and bumps. It wasn't till they were a good distance away that she dared to breathe deeply again.

As they drove into the yard of the depot, the hooter on the roof blew the 'all clear'. She shone her torch on her watch: seven o'clock of a murky November morning. She'd been on active duty fourteen hours. She slumped on the steering wheel, tears of relief and nervous exhaustion streaming down her face. She felt a cold, wet nose in her ear. A little warm tongue licked away her tears.

"Oh, we made it, didn't we?"

She hardly had the strength to lift off her tin hat. She tried it on him and laughed. All she could see was his little black nose.

"How'd you like to be Fireman Bill?"

"Still here, then?"

The milkman, Farmer Heath, grinned at Elsie as he took her jug. It was several mornings after last Thursday's terrible raid on Coventry. Elsie had been on duty again all night. She was ready for bed now, her warm, greatcoat buttoned over her pyjamas. Farmer Heath poured a generous measure of milk into her jug from the churn in the back of his float. He nodded at the house opposite Elsie's.

"Old Mrs Oldham's moved out to her daughters. She's had enough. She says help yourself to the coal left in her coal shed. You're the only one left holding the fort now down this street."

Most of the old Victorian terraced houses on either side were either boarded up or damaged. Only Elsie's and Mrs Oldham's at the bottom of the street next to a high buttressed wall appeared to be intact.

"Do you remember how Mum and Dad hated this factory wall when it first went up? I reckon it saved me quite a bit of bomb damage. Mind you. when I got home in the small hours of this morning, I went to unlock the front door and it wasn't there. It had blown in."

"Where's Fireman Bill? Are you still here?"

Elsie nodded to the front of the float. Toby was licking the hooves of Joey, Farmer Heath's pony. His little tail was wagging fit to drop. He could taste the towpath, scent the Cut, picture Bob.

Farmer Heath's farm bordered the Coventry Canal at Foleshill. He milked his own cows. He sold the fresh milk to the crews of passing boats and all round the village. By then, Foleshill was a suburb of Coventry. But the older inhabitants still referred to it as 'Foleshill Village'.

"Do you take him to the fire station with you?", Farmer Heath asked as they both watched him indulgently.

"Oh, no, we've already adopted two strays and a budgie. All bombed out strays are supposed to be tied up outside the Rest Centre. If they're not claimed by the end of the day, the RSPCA puts them down."

"You reckon old Arky pinched him?"

"Well, probably, look at that collar. Beautifully made. That's woman's handiwork."

"You'd have to make sure you wedge that front door, or he'll be orf."

"Oh, no fear of that", Elsie laughed. "He guards the hay box. So that's what you wanted some of my hay for?" She nodded.

"I found the box in the loft. Mum and Dad must have used it in the First World War. Before I go on duty, I bring a stew and a milk pudding to the boil on the range. Then I bury them in the hay in the hay box. And they go on cooking gently till I get back. Then we have a good hot meal together. It gives me such a welcome when I get home, he flings himself into my arms and kisses me all over. He's a very affectionate little dog. Somebody must be missing him no end."

Farmer Heath banged the lid down on the churn.

"I am getting short of customers. No boats allowed into Coventry again today. The Oxford's still closed from Braunston. They copped a parcel in Braunston Puddle the other day."

He stepped up into the float and gathered the reins.

"Do you think we'll have another raid tonight?"

Elsie nodded.

"Hitler says he is going to finish us off, and then he's going to Coventrate every city in Britain."

"Well, you better get your beauty sleep then", Farmer Heath advised her.

"See you tomorrow"

Elsie smiled.

"God willing."

As Joey the pony picked his way to the top of the deserted street, Farmer Heath glanced back. He caught a parting glimpse of Elsie's erect young figure disappearing into the house with her jug of milk and her little dog. He'd known her all his life. He'd known the struggle her elderly parents had had to raise their one little ewe lamb. How proud old Mr and Mrs Anker would have been now to see their brave daughter.

"Back soon, Fireman Bill", Elsie promised that night, stroking him goodbye as he lay on guard by the hay box. It wasn't only his food he was guarding with his life. It was the hay he didn't want to be parted from. The hay with its captured scents and picture of towpath verges. He had only to close his eyes, rest his nose on his paws against the box and be back home again with his gang and his White City.

The muffled sound of a distant bomb rattled the ornaments on the mantelpiece. The raid had already begun. Elsie wedged the front door in place as firmly as she could. It'll probably be weeks before she could find a carpenter to rehang it properly. She slipped her gas mask over her shoulder, adjusted the strap of her tin hat, drew on her gauntlet gloves and wheeled her despatch bike into the empty street.

The deep thud of another bomb shook through her arms and the soles of her feet. Guns thundered overhead. Though it was pitch dark down in the lee of the big factory wall, the sky between the houses at the top of the street was a fiery red. A huge silvery pink barrage balloon was floating across it. Golden sparks shot across busy searchlight beams. Acrid smoke made her eyes run. The timber yards along the canal must have copped it again.

At the top of the street, she paused to steady the bike and steel her nerve against the racket of planes, guns, bombs, emergency bells.

"If a bomb has my number on it", she told herself, "I just pray I know nothing about it."

Eyes ahead to get her balance, she kicked the engine into life. The bomb fell. Windows smashed, chimneys crashed. Where Elsie and the bike had been seconds before, was only a huge smoking hole. Up from the centre, a water main shot to the sky, sizzling, steaming over the hot earth, hissing over shards of red-hot metal. It gushed, tumbled, swirled, dammed against the wall still standing at the bottom of the street

Toby crouched, terrified, against the hay box. Ornaments lay shattered in the darkness around him. Every hair on end, every whisker a quiver, told him a monster was coming to get him.

Crash! It burst down the door. A wall of icy cold water swept him off his feet. Over went the hay box. He paddled furiously in the darkness. Chairs bobbed up against him. Paddle, paddle. The table turned turtle and floated away. He bumped into walls. Paddle, paddle. Pictures brushed past him. There must be some way out. Once again, he was thrashing, splashing, gasping for his life.

19

Stray

"Want a dog?"

Farmer Heath stroked the little dog he was holding under his arm. Tinker, the travelling blacksmith, stared at the dog and racked his brains.

"Now, where have I seen you before?"

"One of the fire service girls found him in a raid. She was killed two weeks ago. All they found was a bit of number plate off her despatch bike. A week later, a lady in the next street heard a dog barking in the empty house. A burst water main had built up in the kitchen. Eventually somebody must have turned off the main. The water had found its way into an old well under the scullery. He was trapped by a pile of furniture. He was as thin as a herring when somebody's had the meat."

Tinker laughed. Toby was bright as a button now and delighted to see him.

"He looks all right now."

"I had to feed him very careful. Just a little warm water at first, and made sure he kept that down. Later, milk, then gruel, then normal. I can't take him, sir", Tinker said regretfully, "I go to so many places where they have dogs, he wouldn't be welcome."

He frowned again. "I wish I could remember where I've seed him before."

"Well, I can't keep him", Farmer Heath said, because of my sheepdogs."

He fondled Toby's silky ears.

"He's a plucky little thing. For the girl's sake. I want him to go to a good home. It's the least I can do."

At dusk that evening, two little boat girls called at Heath's farm to buy a jug of milk. Nobody saw Toby following them down to the field, into the gathering gloom, to the towpath leading to Coventry Basin.

"Scram! Go 'ome."

They tried to send him back. They were a London boat family. They'd never seen Toby before, knew nothing about the Hone family and their horse-drawn boats. Their sad, but important, mission was to deliver two boatloads of flat-packed coffins to Coventry as soon as possible.

Toby watched dejectedly as their boats chugged away into the bereaved and battered city. He trotted after them into the twilight.

A week later, he found himself tied up in the line of strays outside the Rest Centre. He'd been living rough, scavenging in the ruins of the city, ratting in the broken sewers. He was filthy dirty and stank to high heaven.

It was one of those miserable foggy days in early December when daylight gives up struggling by three o'clock in the afternoon. Toby had given up too. He wasn't even howling. He just sat there, sad-eyed and bewildered, wondering why nobody loved him and everybody was looking at him askance, giving him a very wide berth.

As night fell, only an old collie and Toby were left unclaimed. When the big gloved hands of the RSPCA man lifted him towards the cage in the back of the van, his old spirit suddenly came back. He shot from his grasp and scooted away into the fog. Nose to the ground, he set out along the canal, determined this time to find his towpath.

There was no towpath. He was on the wrong side of the Cut.

20

Winston Churchill

"Well, at least we know he's still alive, Dad."

Betty stood on the lock side, holding Bob, and Jack the mule. Mum and Rose were working the boats through the lock. The boats were packed with sacks of oats for Kench's Mill in Banbury. It was their last trip before Christmas.

Toby had been missing for over seven weeks. There had been several sightings of him reported on the grapevine. Brian had seen him at Hawkesbury Hall. Mr Soden, the travelling fireman, knew all about Elsie and Arky. Tinker had seen him at Heath's farm. Sadly, by the time he remembered which horse he belonged with, Toby had disappeared again. Since then, there had been two more sightings. Somebody had seen him living rough on a derelict boat after the raid on Gas Street Basin in Brummigum. And Suey Beechey had picked him up down the Warwick Canal.

"He were 'itching a lift, Lizzie", Suey told Mum, "I had to look twice to make sure it were 'im. He were that lost and scruffy. I were going to bring him back to you, but he scorted orf."

Suey's boat, the Leam, was different from the White City. It carried liquid gas tar in two tanks under its long, flat deck. She shook her head sadly at Mum.

"He weren't at home on a tar boat, Lizzie."

"If we'd been doing our proper trip instead of puddling along 'ere with oats and beans and what have yer," Betty grumbled, "we'd have found 'im by now."

"Don't you grumble about Farmer Knott's oats, my gal."

Farmer Knott's farm bordered the canal at Wormleighton. In those days, farmers cut their grains still on the stalk, bound it in sheaves and stacked them in ricks. In the winter, a big thrashing drum was towed from farm to farm and thrashed the grain into big hessian sacks.

"Corn to the Co-op, barley to the brewery, oats to the mill, not to mention potatoes", Dad reminded her. "Without Farmer Knott these last few weeks, we'd have had nothing saved up for Christmas."

It was Christmas Eve. Hitler had put off his air raids until Boxing Day. Everyone wondered if he meant it. The Hone family had made their traditional pilgrimage to lay a holly wreath on Granny Rosetta's grave. Then they decorated the tillers of the boats with holly, ivy and old man's beard.

Late in the afternoon, Mum and Rose had gone last minute Christmas shopping on Banbury market. The stall-holders often sold their goods cheaper towards the end of the day, and Mum would find what she called 'bargains'. Betty had stayed with Dad, watching him finish a new rope fender on the table in the cabin of the White City.

It was a week now since anybody had seen Toby.

"Wonder where he is, Dad."

Betty's eyes filled with tears.

"Oh, don't start again", Dad pleaded, struggling with his rope work. "You're as bad as your Mum putting that plank out night after night." Dad missed him too, though he didn't show it. He tried to cheer her up.

" 'ere, 'old this bit of rope for me a minute."

She helped with the rope, but she couldn't stop crying.

"Remember that old bundle of rope I plied for him to play with, when we first had him?" Dad asked kindly.

She nodded, smiling through her tears. "He used to pretend it were his rope rat, tossing, catching, chasing it up and down the empty boat."

Dad nodded. "And how he'd sit, still as still, watching for a real rat, head on one side, eyes bright, ears cocked. He could almost talk with Emmy as Dad, and with his bark, he had quite a different bark for wanting to get on the boat and wanting to get orf."

"He could hunt and swim and dive and doggy paddle."

"Moy hoy yeah, he could doggy paddle."

Dad tapped in the last end of rope and neatly finished the fender. They both fell silent, missing Toby more than ever.

"Look what we found", Mum announced triumphantly as she and Rose arrived back. She unwrapped four cups and set them in a row on the table.

"Real china."

"But they ain't got no 'andles", Dad protested.

"There's a war on, Dad", Rose told him severely, "we has to do without 'andles."

Mum, pleased as punch, held up two lisle stockings - one beige, one black.

"What do you think these are?"

"Odd stockings", said Dad.

"Salvage," Mum beamed, "from bombed out factories. Tuppence a leg from that store down by Tooley's."

She drew out more, all odd, like a conjuror out of a hat.

"Boil them all up together with old tea leaves and they comes out matching. Well, almost."

"Guess who we see down by Tooley's boatyard, Dad?", Rose said, very excited. "Mrs Rolt, Angela. Cressy's still moored out 'Ungerford way. She was ever so pleased to see us. She says Mr Rolt's down in the dumps. He's finished his book about the canals, but nobody wants to print it. They say nobody's interested in canals no more. People won't read it. And anyway, there ain't enough paper for books in wartime."

"Extra rations for Christmas," Mum butted in, dumping the packets on the table. Four ounces of sugar and two ounces of tea per person with love from the Food Office. She snatched up the rest of the packages so Betty couldn't look. You can't see no more, she told her trying to cheer her up.

"Them's presents for you, from Father Christmas."

Even that didn't cheer Betty. All she wanted for Christmas was for Toby to come back.

Late that night, Dad replaced his shaving mug up on the shelf.

"Night Toby", he said to himself, thinking of the real Toby, wherever he might be.

"Put the plank out, Alf", Mum's voice begged from

behind the bed curtain. Dad hesitated. What was the use?

"Please, Alf."

Dad heaved a sigh, and put the plank out.

Early on Christmas morning, Dad opened the cabin doors and nearly fell over something in the hatches. He shone his lantern. A bleary eye lit up. A weary tail wagged.

"It's here!" he yelled.

"Who's 'ere?", Mum asked from the bed.

"Winston Churchill. Who do you think?"

In no time at all, the others pulled coats over their nightgowns and crowded round him. Toby whimpered, longing to lick them all, but he couldn't move. Dad shone the lantern closer. Toby's little legs, filthy dirty, were like matchsticks. Prickly burrs from the verges had knotted and matted into his coat. There was blood everywhere.

"Here's his feets", Mum cried, full of concern. "Look at his poor feets. Red raw."

"He must have walked miles and miles," Rose marvelled.

Betty stroked him gently over and over.

"If only you could talk to us. Toby."

Dad laughed.

"He would be famous then, our Betsy."

"I don't want him to be famous no more", she said quietly, bursting with joy and contentment. "I want him to be just our Toby."

But Toby did become famous.

21

Fame at Last

"Can we have a look, Mister?"

Rose and Betty had been daring each other all afternoon to find out what the little man on the bank was drawing. It was late afternoon on a glorious hot day in September 1943, four years since the war broke out. Rose was 15 and Betty 11. Toby was still their boat dog, and their two boats were still drawn by those inseparable pals, Bob the horse and Jack the mule. They still had to face raids, but the tide of war was on the turn. The secret grapevine had grown to flourish right through Europe. Brave soldiers, including Abe Darby, had died winning back all the territory they had lost in North Africa. There was still talk of invasion, but it was now the invasion to liberate occupied Europe.

The man smiled and showed them the picture. It was a pencil sketch of the White City with Toby peeping over the side.

"That's our Dad's boat", Rose told him, "and that's our boat dog!"

Betty studied the drawing. "You've made his ears smaller."

She didn't know whether to be pleased or sorry.

"Artists are allowed to make ears smaller," he looked at Rose with a twinkle in his eye, "and ladies more beautiful. It's called artistic licence."

Rose blushed. She liked to be treated like a lady, especially by a gentleman. She assumed he was a gentleman. He'd a posh, educated voice like Mr Rolt, and a very trim moustache. It's his collar that didn't fit properly, and he was sitting on the grassy bank like a jolly little gnome.

"You're an artist?", Rose asked.

He nodded. "And a writer and a teacher. I teach at a large boy's school called Rugby."

"A hartist, a writer and a teacher," Betty said, "you must be very clever."

"What's your name?"

She watched him write "Denys Watkins-Pitchford", but she couldn't read it.

"Goes on a bit, don't it?"

He laughed. "My friends call me BB."

"Like our Dad's cartridges", Rose told him.

He was delighted.

"Really? When I was young, I had an old gun called Belching Bess. It took only BB cartridges. So my friends all dubbed me BB."

He inclined his head graciously.

"You may call me BB, if you like."

"I'm Rose, and she's Betty."

"How d'you do, Rose and Betty?"

"That's our boat over there", Rose pointed proudly.

"You're very lucky", he said. "And what's your little dog

called?"

"Toby."

He carried on sketching.

"I had a Toby once, and a Sport, Sparky, Don, Judy, Busy, pet hedgehogs, pet geese, pet birds. I never went to school, you see."

They sank down on the grass beside him in amazement. "How's you learn to read and write?"

"The village schoolmaster tutored me. I was very sickly as a child."

He tugged his collar into place.

"Born without collarbones, among other things. When my brothers went away to school, I was very much alone. I learned to love the countryside and wild animals. Later, I went to art school. Now I teach art, but", he gave a very envious smile, "I'd far rather live on a boat like you and write books and draw pictures."

"Our friend Mr Rolt lives on a boat", Rose told him. "He wrote a book about the canals, but nobody wants to print it."

"Well, this is one of the pictures for Mr Rolt's book."

BB sketched swiftly.

"It is going to be published next year. It's going to be called 'Narrow Boat'. It's a fine book. I'm hoping it will do a lot of good. And I'm proud to be doing the illustrations for it."

Rose was puzzled.

"Why are you doing the pictures?"

BB confessed: "I won a very famous prize for a book I wrote last year. The publishers think if I do the illustrations, more people will buy the book. I think people will buy it because it's a good book. I think Narrow Boat will be a very famous book.

"And will Toby be famous too?" both of them asked.

"Who knows?"

BB gathered up his work.

"Anyway, here's to Toby! God bless him."

"Mum, Dad." They raced back to the White City, bursting to tell them the good news.

"Mr Rolt's book's coming out next year", Rose told them.

"And our Toby's going to be in it, and he'll be famous," said Betty.

"Sshhh." Mum silenced them and Dad held up a stern hand. They looked round, puzzled. As the town hall clock was chiming the hour on the still evening air, all boat families were assembling quietly on their boats and along the quay to listen to the news on the wireless. There was a tremendous air of excitement and expectancy. All who had wirelesses in their cabins had turned up the volume. In all the streets nearby, people had turned up the volume and flung open their windows and their doors so everybody could hear.

"This is the six o'clock news and this is Stuart Hibberd reading it. There is good news. The best news of the war, and John Snagge will read the account."

"Italy has surrendered ...."

The rest of the account was drowned in cheers. People were hugging each other, kissing and crying.

"Is it Muscle Meany, Dad?" Betty asked bewildered. Dad nodded, grinning all over his face.

"Told you he'd be scuppered at the finish".

"Is the war finished, Mum?" Rose asked equally bewildered.

"No, dear. We've a lot more locks to go yet, but we hope it's the beginning of the end."

Everybody stiffened to attention as the national anthem poured out. All over Banbury, all over Britain, doors and windows were flung wide, swelling the strains. Church bells pealed.

In their stable at the Leathern Bottle, Bob and Jack whinnied to each other, wondering what all the racket was about.

And on his cabin top in the midst of all the celebration, wagging for joy, with his tail cut short and his ears all wrong, stood Toby of the White City.

And that's the end of Toby's story. I hope you enjoyed it.

The drawing of Toby of the White City by Denys Watkins-Pitchford - 'BB'
(Part of a larger image published in LTC Rolt's 'Narrow Boat' of 1944)

The Oxford & Grand Union routes from the Midlands to London (1940)
To Coventry
To Leicester
To Birmingham
Braunston Junc
Napton Junc
Braunston Tunnel
Norton Junc
Buckby
Northampton
Wellingborough
River Nene
Jenny Compton
Claydon
Cropredy
Stowe Hill
Gayton Junc
Blisworth Tunnel
Stoke Bruerne
Banbury
Grand Union Canal
Oxford Canal
Somerton
Buckingham
Fenny Stratford
Thrupp
Kidlington
Leighton Buzzard
Oxford
Aylesbury
Marsworth Junc
Abingdon
Wendover
Tring
Grand Union Canal
Kings Langley
Henley-on-Thames
Rickmansworth
Watford
Harefield
River Thames
Slough
Uxbridge
Reading
Regents Canal
R. Lee
Windsor
Brentford
London
Staines
River Thames
Regents Canal Dock
Limehouse Cut

Oxford
George Street
George Street Mews
NUFFIELD COLLEGE AND GARDEN
Worcester Street
Worcester College
Original Oxford Canal Basin
WORCESTER ST. CAR PARK
New Road
Castle Hill
Hythe Bridge Street
Oxford Canal
River Thames
Pacey's Bridge

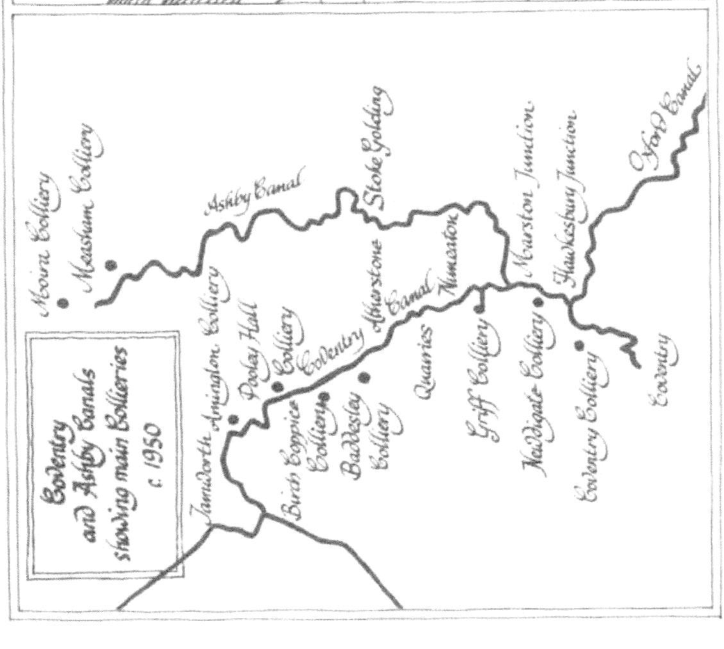
Coventry and Ashby Canals showing main Collieries c. 1950
Moira Colliery
Measham Colliery
Ashby Canal
Stoke Golding
Amington Colliery
Pooley Hall Colliery
Coventry Canal
Atherstone
Nuneaton
Marston Junction
Hawkesbury Junction
Oxford Canal
Tamworth
Birch Coppice Colliery
Baddesley Colliery
Quarries
Griff Colliery
Newdigate Colliery
Coventry Colliery
Coventry

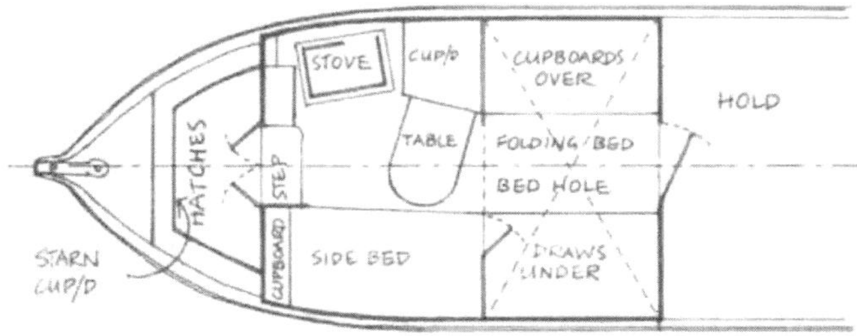

INTERIOR LAYOUT OF HORSE OR BUTTY BOAT

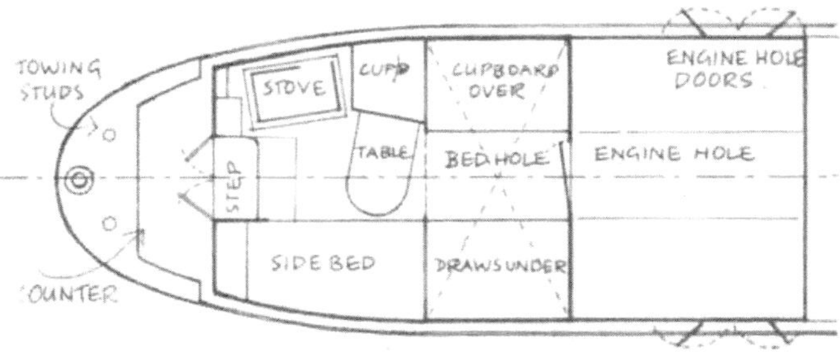

INTERIOR LAYOUT OF MOTOR BOAT

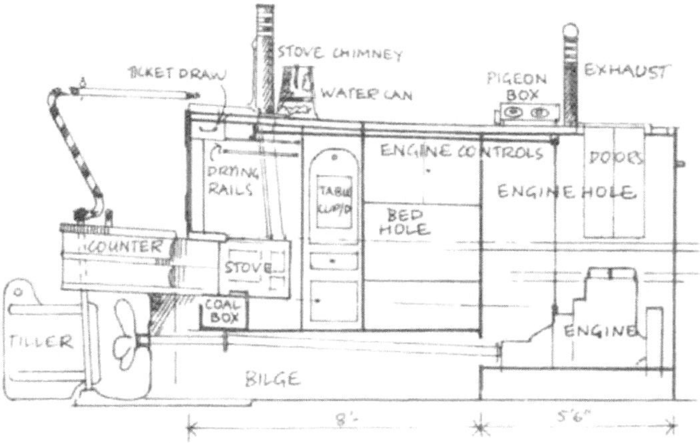

SOME EARLY MOTOR BOATS WERE CONVERTED HORSE BOATS AND HAD THE PROPELLER MORE EXPOSED

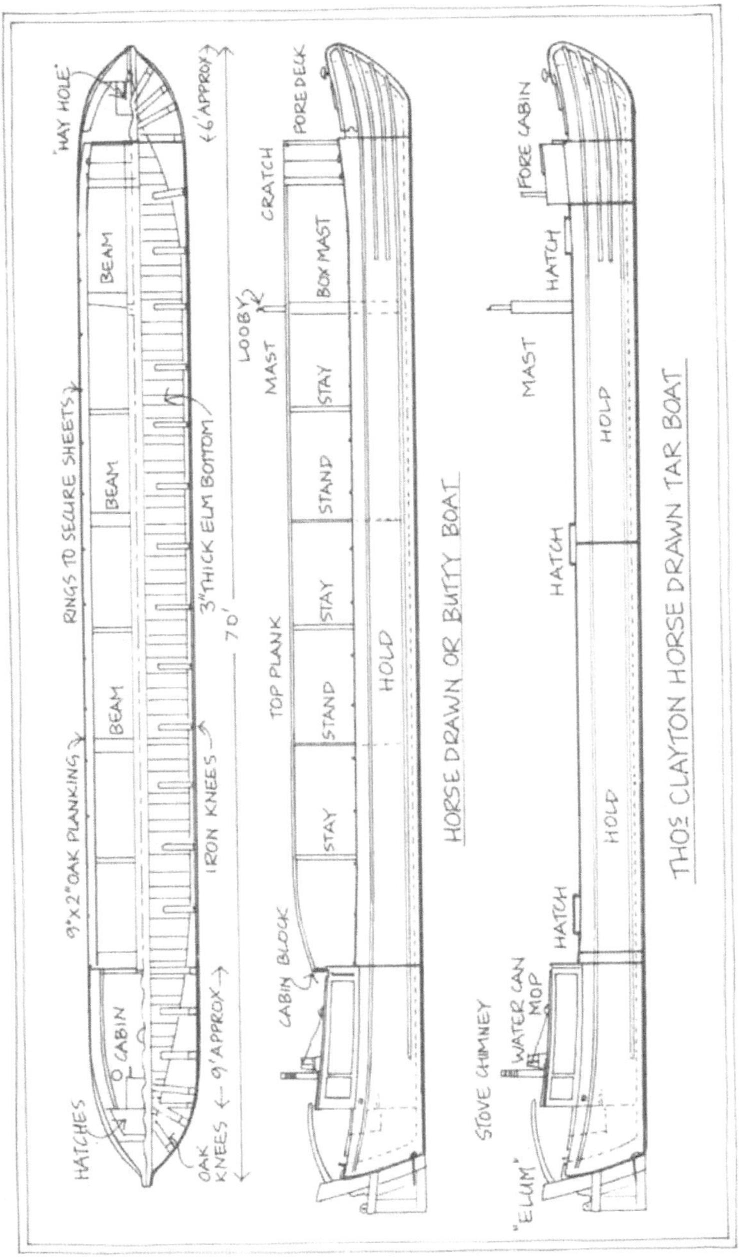
"HAY HOLE"
6' APPROX
RINGS TO SECURE SHEETS
BEAM
BEAM
BEAM
9"x2" OAK PLANKING
3" THICK ELM BOTTOM
70'
IRON KNEES
CABIN
HATCHES
OAK KNEES
9' APPROX
FORE DECK
CRATCH
BOX MAST
LOOBY
MAST
STAY
STAND
STAY
STAND
STAY
TOP PLANK
HOLD
CABIN BLOCK
HORSE DRAWN OR BUTTY BOAT
FORE CABIN
HATCH
MAST
HOLD
HATCH
HOLD
HATCH
WATER CAN
MOP
STOVE CHIMNEY
"ELUM"
THOS CLAYTON HORSE DRAWN TAR BOAT

Also by the same author -

Published by CanalBookShop

Towards the late 1950s, horse-drawn narrow boats became a rarer and rarer sight on Britain's canals. Carrying a wide variety of cargoes to such destinations as the Potteries, the textile mills of Lancashire, the papermills of London, the colleges of Oxford, they struggled on against increasing competition from rail and road traffic to maintain their place in the country's economy. Yet little has been written about the families who lived and worked on these boats - in particular the women.

Drawing on recorded interviews with the few boatwomen left who were born and bred on horse-drawn boats, Sheila Stewart recounted their experiences as seen through the eyes of an illiterate boatwoman, travelling mainly on the Oxford Canal through the Great War, the Depression, the Second World War, and the decline of the canals. It is a poignant account of astonishing courage and resilience, capturing a unique way of life during the first sixty years of the twentieth century.